$10,000 per Income Strategies: Tips, Tricks & Hacks To Wealth Creation And Financial Freedom : Transform Your Lifestyle Within 30 days

© **Healthy Pragmatic Solutions Inc. Copyright 2018 - All rights reserved.**

The contents of this book may not be reproduced, duplicated or transmitted without direct written permission from the author.

Under no circumstances will any legal responsibility or blame be held against the publisher for any reparation, damages, or monetary loss due to the information herein, either directly or indirectly.

Legal Notice:

You cannot amend, distribute, sell, use, quote or paraphrase any part or the content within this book without the consent of the author.

Disclaimer Notice:

Please note the information contained within this document is for educational purposes only. No warranties of any kind are expressed or implied. Readers acknowledge that the author is not engaging in the rendering of legal, financial, medical or professional advice. Please consult a licensed professional before attempting any techniques outlined in this book.

By reading this document, the reader agrees that under no circumstances are is the author responsible for any losses, direct or indirect, which are incurred as a result of the use of information contained within this document, including, but not limited to, — errors, omissions, or inaccuracies.

Introduction….5

Chapter 1: Passive Income……6

Chapter 2: Day Trading For Beginners….26

Chapter 3: Playing It Safe : Long Term Investing….61

Chapter 4: Real Estate….65

Chapter 5: Business Fundamental Principles…133

Chapter 6 Conclusion…189

Introduction

You've probably decided to read this book because your looking for a way to diversify your streams of income and build a more robust portfolio. -And probably most likely interested in passive income right?

This book is designed to inform you about the ins and outs, potential risks and benefits of day trading, dividend investing, real estate and other online business ventures that encompass passive income. And also address myths, misconceptions and ultimately give you realistic and sound business advise.

Whether your looking to leave your job, financial freedom or just learning to create more streams of passive income this is your guide to success. I don't promise you will make a fortune, but I can promise you will become more educated and make better informed decisions.

Chapter 1: Passive Income

Online Business

We've all heard of this term "passive income" better known as the "lap-top lifestyle". But does it really exist? Can you really quit your job and live on the beaches of Bali (city in Thailand) and live the rest of your life through geographical arbitrage?

Well, here are the cold hard facts. -**_Yes and No._** You see to a certain degree income does become passive once you set everything up right and have systems in place that work for you. However, you'll notice that whatever you don't focus on tends to decline in income.

In this day and age ever since the advent of the internet there has been a wave of online entrepreneurs and digital nomads who pitch you this pipe sized dream of living on the beaches and working whenever you want to, and of course trying to sell you their courses. The reality is most these business models leverage off already existing brands that have established authority and millions of ready to buy customers at their disposal.

Also, since you are using the internet your connected to this vast online global market on a whole entirely new scale, and as such you can reach people from all across the globe! Now this is the beauty of online businesses and how it creates this so called " passive income". All you need to do is select a product, run some ads, and do some SEO (search engine optimization) and within a few hours you can expect money to come in, contingent on if you selected the right product and targeted the right audience.

Hence, naive entrepreneurs do this and fall for this notion that they are set for the rest of their lives. But fail to realize that they don't own the customers they are selling to, but the merchant they are leveraging off owns the actual customer. Not only that, but all because you had a good month with a specific product doesn't mean it will last, although the income is passive for that period of time once things are set up, what they fail to realize is passive income doesn't mean **PERMANET income**.

I am emphasizing this fact that passive income does not equate to permanent because I don't want you to fall for that illusion I fell for when I started out. These types of entrepreneurs are the types to make decent incomes of 5-7k per month or perhaps even six figures a year, but once they become complacent, make poor money management decisions and let their business run on "auto-pilot" there income starts to decline and before you know it they are back to working their 9-5s.

You see once you start creating a form of passive income don't become complacent you need to continually look for new business ventures to participate in. This is in order to continue grow your business and preserve your wealth.

A great example of this is a well known affiliate website called click-bank. Entrepreneurs who have become successful afflliates of the many products on this site tend to fall for this illusion that their passive income is permanent, and one day an algorithm shifts or policies change and you lose all your income!

The appropriate way of looking at this type of income should not be considered entirely passive, but leveraged income. Meaning there is a certain degree of minimal work, but you are leveraging systems to work for you in order to create income.

Bottom line is you will have to work no matter what, and people who promise you this passive income lifestyle living on the beach and sipping on martinis for the rest of your life are flat out lying to you!

Real Estate & Stocks

Real estate and stocks are truly the most genuine forms of passive income. These vehicles are truly passive for the most part, but even so are not entirely passive and do require your attention. As you can see here again the "set it and forget it" kind of mentality proves to be false.

If you own a property and lets say you go the extra mile and hire a property manger to manage your property, you still need to monitor what's happening and be involved. What if your property gets damaged or needs repairs, upgrades and renovations? As for stocks you need to monitor if they go up or down, trends, and other things in order to ensure you don't lose the value of your stocks.

You see no matter what vehicle you choose there will always be a certain required effort from your end, even if its minimal, but nothing becomes 100% passive. This is just my honest discourse from my personal experiences on this subject matter.

Bitcoin – The Truth

Bitcoin has been all over media and has bombarded the masses with the concept of a new digital currency that could possibly take over real money. Appealing to people with the concept of wealth transfer from the elite & rich to creating a equitable society. Do I believe in bitcoin or investing in it? Can money be made off bitcoin? – I will answer these following questions.

In 2017 bitcoin sky rocketed in value and there were even some people who were pouring out their life savings in hopes to become the next bitcoin millionaire. A very bold and I would have to say a misinformed move.

So now to address the questions I proposed earlier. Do I believe in bitcoin? In short no, but I do believe in the technology behind it known as "blockchain", but that is a subject matter for another time. You see bitcoin has no intrinsic value like silver or gold, which we can see since ancient times has retained its inherent value over the ages. Companies that divvy out stocks to their shareholders also posses inherent value and this is derived from the product or services that companies provide consumers.

For example, the technology/electronics company Apple has an inherent value derived from its products and services which give their stocks its intrinsic value.

What inherent value does bitcoin posses? The answer is none, and its simply run by a complex algorithm which can easily be duplicated, and since the advent of bitcoin there have been multiple new cryptocurrencies released on the same concept.

Bitcoin is now being regulated by the government and not only that, but is strongly disliked by central banking authorities. I am sure bitcoin will co-exist with our current currency, but I am extremely doubtful that it will ever take over.

You see bitcoin is nothing more than a "bubble" and really is a "pump and dump scheme" that many used to get rich. Meaning bitcoin appreciated in value because people kept throwing their money at it, and thus it started to sky rocket although it had no REAL value!

Can money be made off bitcoin? Yes, absolutely! But, you are unlikely to become a millionaire through it unless you were one of the first to invest in it back in ***2008-2014.*** I would not recommend investing your money in any cryptocurrency due to the volatility and uncertain nature of this new type of currency. The people who made their fortune were the lucky ones, and have probably moved on to other sustainable business ventures with all the capital bitcoin provided for them.

My take away message is don't fall for fads or trends, if you truly want to become wealthy and stay rich you need to invest in things that last and not get rich quick schemes.

Passive Income Business Models:

*Below is a list of passive income business models I have named for you and described to give you a better picture.

- ***Print On Demand (POD) T -shirts*** – This service requires you to upload a apparel/clothing designs and when customers purchase an item than a t- shirt is produced and shipped to the customer, and you receive a royalty from what the customer paid the merchant. -Minus production costs. You don't deal with inventory or shipping, you only upload designs!

- ***Publishing Print On Demand*** - Similar to how print on demand t-shirts works, you upload your manuscripts, covers, etc and when a customer purchases a book it is than printed and shipped to the consumer, and than you receive a royalty from what the customer paid. -Minus production costs. You don't deal with inventory or shipping if it is a print on demand business model.

- **Affiliate Marketing** - You become an affiliate of a larger brand and endorse a product that already exists, and all you do is drive traffic to the product you are selling and once that product is sold you receive a commission based on the terms of agreement. You don't deal with inventory, shipping, etc. That's all taken care by the vendor. All you need to do is market the product successfully and close sales.

- **Drop Shipping** - Find a reputable supplier and create your own website. Once a customer has made a purchase on your site you than take that money and buy the product from the supplier and you profit off the difference. The supplier deals with the shipping and inventory. So all your doing is being the middle man facilitating transactions, and buying low and selling high to make a profit. A well known website platform you can use to host your products on is "Shopify".

I am going to share with you information no other passive income guru does! – You see every other book that claims to teach you about passive income leaves a lot of crucial information out, such as suppliers and where to find freelancers to for a fraction of retail value.

Not only will I provide you the DIRECT source, but will mention the company's where you can start signing up to use their products or services to start your online business ventures.

Where To Start Your Online Business - Platforms

Print On Demand - Tee-spring, Etsy, Printful, Redbubble, Tee-fury, Merch

Publishing – Kindle, Kobo, Ingram sparks, publishing drive, Draft 2 Digital, Scrbid, Tolino, Barnes & Noble, Google Play, and Apple

Affiliate Marketing – Clickbank, JVzoo, ShareASale, PeerFly

Drop shipping - Shopify, Pinnacle Cart, LemonStand, 3dcart

Where To Find Suppliers & Freelancers

Alibaba - For drop shipping

Alibaba express - For drop shipping

Fiverr – For publishing (print on demand)

Upwork – For publishing (print on demand)

Elance - For publishing (print on demand)

Toptal - For publishing (print on demand)

Design Pickle - print on demand (T-shirts)

99 designs – For print on demand (T-shirts)

Bing ads – For affiliate marketing

Facebook ads – For affiliate marketing

Google ads words - For affiliate marketing

Yahoo Gemni – For affiliate marketing

- The above mentioned freelancing services & suppliers are websites you can check out at your convenience to find a profitable product or services that you can utilize for your online ventures too!

All these online gurus/expert you find on YouTube trying to sell you their course and give you little to no insight on how to get started prior. They withhold critical information from you, and well, you can thank me for saving you hundreds of dollars because all the information I just provided, especially the supplier/freelancer information is the exact same that these gurus sell you in their courses.

Yep. That's right all of these mentioned websites is where everyone get's their work outsourced for cheap and than they bring that product or service to big selling platforms to sell too and make royalties off. Ingenious right?

The thing is to get started you will need some start up capital and once you start operating successfully and making profits you use those same profits to scale up your business by re-investing profits. -Rinse and repeat. Remember feed the business and the business will feed you. I recommend anywhere between ***$1,000 -$3,000 in start up capital to begin with***.

I do not have the time to cover every single online business model in depth due to the nature of this book and all the other topics I cover extensively, but as a courtesy and to keep you satisfied I will go into in depth into detail for one business model, and teach you the ins and outs from beginning to end.

Blueprint) For Print on Demand (T-shirt) Online Business Model

1. Select a print demand platform. Sign up and add your personal and banking information so you can get paid.

2. Sign up for "Merch informer". This service is very cheap and will provide you ideas and good niche selection for you to design a T-shirt. If you don't want to pay and do it yourself than you will need to research trends and niches based on seasonal themes, news, media, and cultures. You can try using google analytics, youtube, foxmetrics or clicky.

3. For design creation there are two ways to go about doing this. If your good with adobe photo shop or have an artistic talent you can simply

create T-shirt by designing images yourself to save you costs. Note they must follow the dimensions the platform you selected uses. Number two is outsourcing and you can do this by using the following freelancing websites I recommend design pickle (flat rate unlimited designs) , 99 designs, or Fiverr. Depending on which freelancing site you choose there are some rules and regulations to follow, but they more or less work the same. You will have to brainstorm ideas based on your research and give instructions of how you want a particular design to look. After that you just wait for your order to be complete which should take around 48-72 hours or even longer depending on your designer and volume of orders. Once you receive your design you will be able to take a final look at it and request changes if necessary, but if your satisfied with the quality of your order simply approve.

4. **BONUS TIP:** Design Pickle has an absolutely FREE no risk 2 week trial for their service. This means you can sign up and complete as much orders as you can within a 2 week period, and than if your not at all satisfied you can ask for your money

back. Note: they will charge your credit card in order for you to get started with the free 2 week trial, but at the end of your trial offer you can just send them an email stating you were not satisfied with the service if it wasn't up to par. Or you can continue using their services at their premium rates if you are happy with the service.

5. Now that you have your design ready to go you upload it to the selling platform you've selected earlier. Some key things to do to maximize your chances of success and selling your t-shirts: you will have to select strategic keywords meaning use search engine optimization (SEO), basically use keywords people are looking for in your product title and description. Speaking of description, you must make a compelling sales page using your copywriting skills. Another thing to note when creating your designs you should have in mind you are trying to create a brand because brands sell for the long term, and trendy t-shirts although extremely profitable taper off. Remember you are a content creator who is trying to sell t-shirts people WANT. The operative word here is "want" and I am emphasizing this as I see a lot of novices create t-shirts on things their passionate about, yet the market doesn't care nor want those types of products. So remember to please research your customers before even designing your first t-shirt!

6. Trademark infringements and violations. You need to do your due diligence with trademark infringements and ensure your designs are not violating any trademarks or copyrights for that matter. You can use websites like www.uspto.gov/trademark (free) or extensions for google chrome like "trademark hunt"(paid service) which find trademarked items for you. It is your responsibility to ensure you are not violating any active trademarks when uploading your designs. The last thing you want is to lose your royalties or have your account blocked. So please remember to do your due diligence, and this applies for phrases and words too!

7. If you have successfully uploaded your design and know without a shadow of a doubt you are in the clear and have complied with all the rules, than all you need do now is wait for your T-shirts to be purchased from customers and you are paid royalties usually between 30-60 days after purchase month. Now just rinse and repeat the process and create your clothing empire! I should also note external advertising helps too,

such as Facebook, Pinterest, Instagram and any other traffic source you can think of that can help promote your t-shirt. I mentioned earlier about creating a brand, and establishing authority on external platforms like Instagram might really help ramp up sales. You create a page dedicated to t-shirts or niche (t-shirts people would want to wear) and than just drop a link on Instagram to the site on where they are sold. Simple right?

This is basically the blueprint on running your own online print on demand clothing business. The best part is you don't have to do deal with any inventory, but only upload designs! Courses charge you hundreds of dollars on the instructional information I have provided and I just gave you that information at a fraction of the cost!

Why Blogs Alone Don't Make You Money $$

There's a big misconception with blogging and making money online . Can you really make a living as a blogger? I will clarify the myths and misconceptions in this section. You see blogs alone if not monetized correctly won't make you money! Regardless of what niche you have selected without a clear cut monetization strategy in place you will not make any money.

Whether it's a fitness blog, how to do stuff, review of products or leisure activities without having some sort of monetization strategy in place and without explicitly selling anything you will not make any money. Depending on google ad sense or any other paid per click advertisement you place on your site should be thought of as an additional revenue stream, and not your main source of monetization.

As on average PPC advertisements for google ads give you 10 cents per click and you can do the math with how much traffic you will need to make anything substantial and worthwhile. So the question is how do you extract substantial amounts money from the traffic on your blogs?- Simply adding value is not enough without having a way to make money off your blog.

There are a few ways you can monetize your blog. The first thing you need to realize is you need to position yourself the right way. Right from the get-go you need to establish to your viewer you are selling or endorsing a product or service. This "something" must solve the problem of the viewer and thus they will be inclined to buy from you.

For instance, you write a blog on how to lose weight and you provide them tips, recipes and workout routines to use. You see if you just leave it as that you are leaving money on the table and that's what I see a lot of inexperienced online marketers do. The right way of doing this is provide the value (tips, recipes, workout routines) and than refer them to an affiliate link or product you own that is related, such as exercise equipment, supplements, protein shakes and recipe books. People are more inclined to buy from you when you give them value first and sell them after. This is how I've personally generated thousands of dollars easily, but I wouldn't suggest to start off with blogging personally unless you can find out a way to outsource it as it can be time consuming.

The next way to monetize your blog is more subtle and I've personally used it as well. You do what is called a "product review" and I recommend you choose a high ticket item such as BBQ, boats, lawn mowers, mentorship packages, marketing services, computers and other electronics. After you give your honest review of a particular product or service you than link your recommended products/services with your affiliate link for them to buy from. Product review blogs are extremely profitable and are one of the best converters when it comes to making money with blogging. Its your choice to mention if your links are affiliate links or not, but you don't have too. Doing your research is essential before you start a blog because you want to write about content that people are interested and are actively looking for. Using SEO would be a good idea too!

CHAPTER 2: Day Trading For Beginners

My Day Trading Strategies

First off before I begin my discourse I must address two universal terms you must familiarize yourself with and become acquainted to when dealing with any types of trades. Please see the following two terms..

Bullish – means a stock or the overall market will go up/increase.

Bearish – means a stock or overall market will go down or decrease.

I target the volatile stocks as making money from this is derived from stocks that are moving up, thus you will want to select stocks that have the potential to rise in value. How do we do this? We need to take a look at press releases, quarterly earnings, and any other types of reliable sources and preferably business news.

For example in Canada a bank called BMO invests 250 millions dollars in a weed company, and weed is set to be legalized within the next few months of this investment. Things like this should tip you off on what to invest in and what not to invest in. You will need to be very analytical. In this case study, government regulations shows a green light for weed and on top of that a bank which is apart of the federal government is publicly investing money into it. These are some things to always keep in mind and monitor while day trading.

You want to focus on liquidity and to do this you need to focus on volume. Meaning when its high peak with a lot of volume that's the best time to start day trading, but when there isn't enough volume it becomes harder to get in and out of stocks effortlessly.

Before getting into investing your first dollar into any stocks I want to you to keep in mind that there is ALWAYS risk involved, and your job as a day trader is to take "measured risks", and you want to find low risk entry stocks. That's the hard part trying to figure out and predict which stocks will move up in value. – Remember there is never a guarantee and day trading is always shrouded in risk.

So you need to have a good "profit setup" in order to play this game right. I'll elaborate, if your risking $100 to make $400 in return that's considered a good profit setup with a 4:1 profit win/lose ratio. Meaning your risking $100 with the potential to make $400. I'll give you an example of a bad profit setup, you invest $100 to make $50 this is a negative ratio and one you shouldn't take!

Were always looking for low risk entries in order to maximize our profits. You must be able to identify good profit setups with the highest potential of profit, but lowest risk of entry. – The key elements to pull this off is to continuously search the market for volume and volatility.

Day trading will require quick decision making, analytical prowess, and focus. I would also go on to say and should mention it requires a lot of mental toughness or stamina because there will be times you will undergo a lot of stress, perhaps a stock plummets in value into a deep valley, but within a few weeks sky rockets higher than ever before. – Patience is a virtue and will need to be exercised during day trading. But you also need to learn how to call it a loss if there is no sign of picking up.

How To Find Profitable Day Trades?

I look for ongoing patterns within the market. I bide time and wait, when the right opportunity presents itself I strike and go into a good profit setup. Resources to use for this, I personally use 5 minute candle stick charts, Moving Averages, Bollinger Bands, Momentum Oscillators, and Relative Strength Index.

Candle stick charts – depict open or closed trades, high volume and low volume. Consisting of red and green candles. The open on the green candles is always the low and for the red is the opposite.

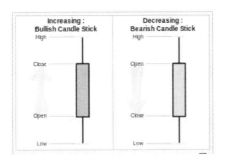

Moving Averages - this is a calculation made by adding up a stock prices over a certain period of time and dividing that total by the total number of periods. For example, in a 5 day period you would add up the prices of Neptune Technologies stocks for those 5 days, ***5+7+9+6+7 =34, 34 divided by 5*** <u>= 6.8 moving average</u>.

Bollinger Bands – These bands are found on a stock chart and are considered "volatility bands", there are upper bands, middle bands and lower bands, and they move according to the volatility in the market. For instance, when volatility increases the bands widen and when volatility decreases the bands narrow. The area above the moving average is called the "buy channel" and the area below the moving average is called the " sell channel". Prices shown in the buy channel region are above the moving average and thus imply a upward trend. Conversely prices shown below the sell channel region show a declining trend.

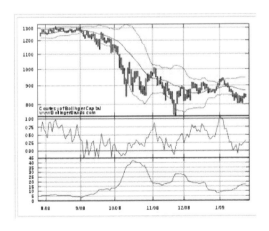

***Bollinger band example**

Momentum Oscillators - Oscillator developed by George C. Lane in the late 1950's. This can help determine when a currency pair is overpurchased or oversold. Thus, traders can view these changes and trends on their chart.

Relative Strength Index – Measures the magnitude of recent price changes to analyze either overbought or oversold conditions. Its mostly used to help identify conditions of either oversold or overbought when trading an asset.

Pattern Trading How It Works?

Once you get use to viewing candle stick charts you'll start to pick up on patterns and trends, and once you can do this effortlessly you will identify the apex point which is also known as the breakout or breakdown point, and at this point you will buy the stock. This is also known to some as momentum styled trading because your leveraging off the momentum that is being created and buying at its apex.

Institutional Trader Vs Private Trader

Institutiona Traders :

- They don't trade for income
- They are paid by corporations to trade other people's money or mange their money.
- More aggressive
- Size of trades are in the millions much larger trade volume transactions
- Accountable to their bosses and report to them

Private Traders:

- Trade for income
- Size of trade is generally in the thousands of dollars
- Has autonomy. Unlike institutional traders who have someone to answer to because they are managing their accounts, private traders don't

have this obligation because they don't manage other people's accounts.

Penny Stocks For Beginners

In this section I will cover the basics of penny stocks and the fundamental underlying principles to making money with them. You've probably heard about people making millions off penny stocks in the news at some point in your life, and well although this is possible it is very unlikely you will be able to replicate the same results.

The purpose of this entire book is to show you fundamentals of different wealth creation vehicles and if your able to master all of them there is a pretty good chance you can hit the 10k per month mark combined with all the strategies which include real estate, dividends, options, online businesses and of course penny stocks.

Now to get back to the topic at hand, what exactly are penny stocks? Penny stocks are known as common public shares of smaller companies that are valued less than a dollar. In the USA penny stocks are considered a security which trades for less than $5 USD per share.

The nature of penny stocks is actually extremely volatile meaning they are prone to extreme fluctuations, dips and dives. -The people who have made their fortunes off penny stocks successfully leveraged the volatility aspect of this type of stock investment. Penny stocks are considered "high risk" investment with low trading volume, meaning there is a higher risk associated with these types of stock and there is not massive demand for them generally speaking as indicated by their low trade volume. These types of stocks don't really appeal nor attract the attention of high end investor, but on the contrary investors tend to neglect and overlook these kinds of stocks.

There are mixed answers that can be found all over the net and media on penny stocks. Some people say that penny stocks is your get rich quick scheme, while others say it's a sure way to lose out on all your money. But what is the truth? – Well, the truth herein lies somewhere in between both answers and in fact there is a certain degree of truth to each of the above sentiments. I guess you could say the truth is the middle road or path per se.

The key is to find quality picks that are valued under $5 USD and this is the tricky part. As it requires an extensive research effort in order to find something worthwhile. - Its not as easy as some may think of simply going on google and searching for the most profitable penny stocks. But in actual fact takes a lot of analysis, critical thinking, and even instinct.

In order to win you need to focus on your small victories or gains as they do add up over time. Remember don't get hung up on the losses, but keep a clear mind and learn from mistakes. Trade cautiously and always be leery and I don't suggest you "double down" or go "all in", instead take your time and get the hang of trading penny stocks for the long run.

There are a lot of so called experts in stock trading who admonish you to go big or go home. But, the statistical data available is indisputable in regards to the winners produced vs losers. There are more losers than winners, so I suggest you play the cautious game as oppose to being overly aggressive.

Aim to make 10% profits per trade and always be cognizant you can LOSE. Knowing this sobering truth of potential losses will prevent you from making more aggressive moves that can cause you to lose everything. Do I feel bad sometimes when I'm on the money and I've only made a 10% profit gain? -No. I am fine with the small wins as they add up over time and I know even if I was right there was potential for me to be wrong.

So how do you find profitable penny stocks? You will need to analyze trends, patterns, industries, media, adapt and even observe what works with other penny stock traders.

There are a few things you are going to have to familiarize yourself with if you want to master penny stocks or at least become experienced. I will go over these fundamentals briefly and note some of these we have previously discussed.

Fundamentals to Penny Stocks

-Candle Stick Charts

- Resistance

- Volume

-Moving Averages

-Stochastics

-VWAP

-Float

-Support

Candle Stick Charts- Depict open or closed trades, high volume and low volume. Consisting of red and green candles. The open on the green candles is always the low and for the red is the opposite.

Resistance - When viewing a stock chart the point of resistance acts like a ceiling and price of stock stalls and drops back down in value. For instance, if there are a high volume of sellers and the price cant breakthrough, than the price will reverse backdown. Essentially, resistance is when you have an overcrowded amount of sellers that overpower buyers which causes the value of that stock to drop in price.

Volume – Is the total amount of stocks traded within the entire market in a specific period of time.

Moving Averages – this is a calculation made by adding up a stock prices over a certain period of time and dividing that total by the total number of periods. For example, in a 5 day period you would add up the prices of Neptune Technologies stocks for those 5 days, ***5+7+9+6+7 =34, 34 divided by 5* = 6.8 moving average.**

Again to summarize moving averages please see below

Day 1 = 5, Day 2 =7, Day 3 = 9, Day 4 = 6, Day 5 =7

Total stock price value = 34

Total number of days within period = 5

34 divided by 5 = ***6.8 moving average***

Stochastics - Is a momentum oscillator developed by George C. Lane in the late 1950's. This can help determine when a currency pair is over purchased or over sold. Thus, traders can view these changes and trends on their chart.

VWAP - Stands for volume weighed at average price. This is a trading bench mark and is calculated by adding up dollars traded for every transaction (price (x) times number of shares traded), and than dividing by total number of shares traded for the day.

Float – Number of shares available for trading.

Support – The opposite of resistance. When viewing a stock chart the point of support acts like a floor and stock prices rise back up. This happens when there is more buying that occurs and that overpowers the selling. The support level is known when buyers start purchasing or enter into a stock.

Risk Management

Whether your dealing with penny stocks, online businesses or even real estate there is always a certain degree of risk involved. The key principle to trading penny stocks is mitigating or managing your risks by taking measured ones. Always anticipate the possibility of loss and know that there is no single guarantee. You must develop what I call a risk-reward ratio and this simply is a measure of weighing your wins to losses.

My standard recommended method of operation is a 1:2 risk-reward ratio. So for instance if your aiming for 10 cents per share (gains), than you should only be willing to risk 5 cents a share (loss). Following this standard rule will save you from the pitfalls that many traders fall into because they got to overly confident.

Remember small consistent gains is the goal here and not "home run hits" or "lottery wins". You want to grow your portfolio over time, and slow and steady wins the race. However, this doesn't mean that you can't take advantage of profitable stocks that are moving extremely well. By all means do your due diligence and leverage stocks that move well, but don't force it! – Go with the flow.

You will also need to learn the skill of cutting your losses quickly. When things start going down south do not keep trying to trade to win back all your losses. Cut your losses and move on! Remember if you lose all your funds you are finished. Thus, you need to develop a strategy and preserve your capital, plan when to sell, buy, and hold ahead of time.

Factors To Look For Before Investing In Penny Stocks

-Stocks are moving in premarket

-Good volume

- Low float

- Some sort of news or catalyst

Market Trading Hours, Times, Schedule

Premarket trading – trade time occurring between **4:00 AM - 9:30 AM**

Day trading hours trade time occurring - **Mon – Fri 9:30 AM – 4:30 pm**

NASDAQ trading hours - Pre-Market Trading Hours from **4:00 AM - 9:30 AM,** Market Hours from **9:30 AM-4:00 AM, 4:00 PM-8:00 PM,** After-Market Hours from **4:00 PM - 8:00 PM**

OTC trading- When trading is done directly between two parties and does not use the supervision of a stock market exchange.

Tools

You will need to utilize scanners which is a tool that searches the stock market according to the set criteria you are using to filter desired results.

Recommended scanner: ***Equity Feed***

Find Like Minded People -Join Facebook Groups

Don't try starting this endeavor of trading alone I strongly recommend you join a Facebook group. Just simply search "stock trading support" or " stock investing group" and you will see thousands suggestions populate. I suggest you choose closed knitted groups, but at the same time you want to have a good amount of traffic there too. I would suggest joining groups in the sizes between 500-3000 people. – Don't get scammed as there may be people in certain groups trying to sell you stuff that is nothing but fluff. So just be aware of your surroundings and do your due diligence.

Dividend Investing

Now lets talk about dividend investing you've probably heard it's a more pragmatic and stable way of investing your money. You receive payments in shareholder dividends month after month or quarter after quarter depending on the corporate structure of the company's dividend stock you purchased.

The positive side to this type of investing is you get to watch compounding interest at work for you. Investing in dividends can be rewarding, but lets get into the good and the bad of this type of investment.

Let's start off with the cons. You see when you invest into dividend stocks you are not in any way guaranteed to be paid, if a company is experiencing a decline or problems with business the dividend payment to you might be reduced, suspended or terminated for an indefinite period of time.

The next problem with dividend investing is taxes! - That's right taxes! Taxes consume most of your profits from your yields. Also to add to that dividend investing generally speaking have little to no capital appreciation within the first 5-7 years.

Now lets talk about the positives of dividend investing. If you do your research and select a good company to buy dividend stocks from you can expect to earn money on a monthly and quarterly basis. – In the next chapter I will discuss the types of dividends stocks you can start investing in. (chapter 3)

The next positive aspect to dividend investing is companys that are established and who have continual growth tend to increase their dividend payouts to you, which simply means more money in your pockets.

Last but not least one of the greatest reasons to invest into dividends stocks is because you get to participate in investing into a proven brand name assuming you are selecting reputable companies to invest in such as Coca-Cola, AT&T, Kimberly Clark, etc. These are companies that have track records of success and have built brand, value, authority and presence in the marketplace.

Ultimately, if you don't have a large volume of cash to invest in dividends (in the millions) I can tell you that you will not get rich off this type of investing. You really need to have money to make money with this type of investment.

Trading Options

Top Option Trading Brokerages

- E*TRADE - Best for options overall.
- Interactive Brokers - Lowest commissions.
- TD Ameritrade - Best options tools.
- TradeStation - Well-rounded offering.
- Charles Schwab - Best for order types.
- Fidelity- Active Trade Pro– I personally use this

*You will need to sign up with these brokerages in order to start trading options. But first I recommend you finish this section of the book on options before creating an account and refer back to this section if you get stuck once your online.

Options is another form of stock trading with low capital, high risk and of course high reward. First off I want to advise if you're a beginner I highly recommend you start off with paper trading! Options are something you must get comfortable with and gain experience in before you start divvying out real cash. I don't want you to waste your money while in the learning process, so please do yourself a favor and start off with paper trading for options. To understand options you have to react to the "bid and asking" movement in relation to the stock you are trading.

What Is An Option?

There are various definitions you can find on the internet of what is an option? Some are very convoluted, but for the purpose of this beginner's guide I will keep things simple and break things down at a fundamental level.

An option is simply an "agreement" between a buyer and seller. This agreement involves both the buyer and seller, giving the buyer the right and seller an obligation to sell and buy the stock at a later date, and at a certain price point.

Where this diverges from traditional stock trading is you are actually looking to predict the future price of an option stock and looking for the "future price" is the basis of the trade.

1 contract is equivalent to 100 shares.

When you have an option order there is going to be 4 fundamental things you will see.

- *Buy to close*
- *Buy to open*
- *Sell to open*
- *Sell to close*

If you see that the stock is bullish (increasing up) you will be "buying calls", and if you observe the stock is bearish (declining) you are buying put. The take away here is your paying a premium for unlimited potential reward, and mitigated risk.

What Is An Option Chain?

Below is the components that make up an option chain..

Volume – contract in current day trades.

Open Interest – Volume of remaining contracts that have not yet been executed. -when an investor bought a stock sometime ago and is still holding, and has yet to close out.

Delta +/- increase or decline of the option price relative to the movement in stock value.

Theta- Time decay, loss of value or drop in price of option per day.

Gamma - measures rate of change in Delta

Vega – The measure of changing volatility

Strike price - are fixed in the option contract that allow the option holder to purchase the stock at the strike price up to its expiration date.

Now your probably confused with all this new terminology? I will simplify all these in an example below to give you a more comprehensive understanding.

Example:

Imagine you had a stock valued at **$1.**

The Delta is at .2 of that stock. (20%), thus if the stock goes up by $1 ($1 total) this means the value of the option I have is going to increase by 20 cents. So if the stock value goes down from $1 to 0.9 than the delta will go decline 0.2, 20 cents.

(Continued using the delta example above) If gamma goes up .1 (value of stock becomes $101)than delta changes to .3 and stocks moves up $1. Now if the stock value goes down to $0.90 than delta will be .1. Remember this is directly related to delta, and delta indicates the increase or decline of an option price relative to the movement of the stock value.

Theta is the loss of value in a stock per day. Let's say theta was 0.06 this means that the option would lose a value of 6 cents per day.

Example of strike price scenario. Imagine Apple has a $5 strike price, over the lifetime(until expiry date) of this option contract, the holder has the ability to exercise purchasing shares for $5 each and let's say the holder buys 50 shares, which is $250. If the Apple value rises to $10 per share, the holder can exercise his/her right to purchase share at $5 and sell it in the open market for $10. In this scenario the option holder would make $500 if he/she sold the 50 shares, which is a $250 profit.

Now if you haven't already I want you to sign up with one of the following brokerages and than come back.

Top Option Trading Brokerages

- E*TRADE - Best for options overall.
- Interactive Brokers - Lowest commissions.
- TD Ameritrade - Best options tools.
- TradeStation - Well-rounded offering.
- Charles Schwab - Best for order types.
- Fidelity- Active Trade Pro– I personally use this

Now that you've selected your trading brokerage lets begin. Now the layouts should be similar, but some will differ from others, but nonetheless the fundamentals should be there.

I know it looks intimidating, but don't let it scare you. I am going to walk you through this step by step.

Last	Chg	Bid	Ask	Vol	Open int	Delta			

theta	Gamma	Vega	Strike						

CALLS	PUTS

*For your reference

So your screen is populated with a whole bunch of information right now. Don't get overwhelmed I am going to break this down and simplify this for you.

Your going to have 11 important columns your going to want to pay attention to and I have created a table for you above for you to reference to. I am going to be showing you the important tabs you will need to focus on in order to grasp the entire picture. For now disregard all other information and let me explain what each of these columns mean.

*I should also mention that a lot of options may have a lot of expiration dates that vary week to week.

(refer back to last page tables if needed)

So right away your going to see two main tabs "CALLS" & "PUTS", you should see calls on the left side and puts on the right side. In the middle area you should see on the sub column a tab called "strike".

Now lets look at the entire sub column tabs. So let's take a look, we will start off with the "last" column and this indicates the percentage of change compared to yesterday. The "Bid & Ask" I've already spoken about earlier so it should be straight forward.

The volume column as previously discussed is the amount of current contracts traded within the day. The Open interest column is contracts that have not yet been exercised.

The delta column is the increase or decrease of an option relative to a 0.1 move in the stock. Than we have time decay theta, which is the drop in value of option price each day if all else remains the same.

Than we have the gamma column which measures the direct rate of change of delta. So whether delta increases or decreases the gamma column will measure by how much. So if delta increases by 0.4 gamma column will indicate 0.4 increases and vice versa if it declines.

Lastly, we also have the "vega" column which measure the changing volatility of the stock.

Now this may take time for you to grasp, so I recommend you go back and forth cross reference materials from the book to your screen to comprehend the concept. Don't get discouraged take it a step at a time.

I also wanted to note, if you are simply "day trading" literally meaning in and out within a day all of this discussed is irrelevant to you. But if you are day trading within extended periods of times such as weeks, months etc it is best to familiarize yourself with all the columns.

FAST In & Out Day Trading

Fundamentals of FAST Day Trading:

- Quick
- Greek Columns irrelevant
- Liquidity – how easy shares of a stock can be converted into cash
- Tight Bid & Ask
- SPY VS PLCN
- Must be focused
- Rational thinking
- Disciplined under pressure
- Capacity to make your own predictions
- Strike price in or out 1 of the money – strike prices are fixed in the option contract that allow the option holder to purchase the stock at the strike price up to its expiration date.
- Sell stock while its moving in your direction (bullish)

So let's say you've purchased a stock. This stock value is now bullish I would strongly suggest as soon as you see that 1 point move you should sell immediately, you could possibly be leaving money on the table in this scenario because there is potential that the stock value keeps rising and if you wait to sell you can potentially maximize your gains. But, you should be willing to sacrifice this due to the fact the opposite may occur as well. Meaning the stock value is bullish for a short period and than starts to become bearish (declines) rapidly and at that point you lost your opportunity to make a quick exit with a tidy profit. – This in essence is quick in and out day trading, characterized by quick entries and exits.

Insider Info

In order to make big gains you will need to be able to access insider info whether that's reading quarterly earning reports, press releases, business news, and even better associating with option private groups made up of experts where you pay them a fee per month to be apart of the group and receive insights for trading options. This will give you the upper edge in trading options, and a much needed one. Make sure the group is reputable so you can rely on their information.

Chapter 3: Playing It Safe : Long Term Investing

In this section I will discuss more conservative styled investing, in particular investing in stocks for long term wealth. Most these stocks will payout dividends quarterly, monthly, annually etc, but keep in mind are subject to change as well. I will give you a breakdown and my top recommended stocks for you to invest in. I give you the stocks I have personally have invested in.

You will have to set up a brokerage account from wherever you live to begin. Once this is done you can start buying and selling stocks.

Conservative Stocks To Invest In:

- BMO – Bank Of Montreal
- TD Bank
- Apple Inc
- Shopify Inc
- Sun Life Financial Inc
- Shaw Communication Inc
- TELUS Corporation Inc
- Exchange Income Corporation
- Exco Technologies LTD
- ALTGAS LTD
- Algonquin Power & Utilities Corp
- Canopy Growth Corporation
- Enecare Inc
- Fortis Inc
- Vecima Network Inc
- Canadian National Railway Co
- Gibson Energy Inc
- Medreleaf Corp
- Manulife Financial Corp
- Emera Inc
- Transalta Renewables Inc
- Inter Pipe Line LTD
- My Food Group Inc
- Sylogist LTD
- Auroa Cannabis Inc
- Emerald Health Therapeutics Inc

- ENG House systems LTD
- Capital Power Corporation
- Vanguard S&P 500 Index ETF TR Unit
- Horizons Marijuana
- Brookfield Infrastructure Partner LP Units
- Riocan real estate investment trust units
- Chartwell Retirement Residence TR unit
- H & R Real Estate Investment Trust Stapled Units
- American Hotel Income Prop REIT LP Units
- Boardwalk Real Estate Invt Trust Units
- Boyd group Income Fund Trust Unit
- Nexus Real Estate
- Moreguard North American Residential Real Estate
- Facebook Inc
- Alphabet inc
- Tesla Inc
- Alibaba Group Inc
- Johnson & Johnson
- Intel Corp
- Wells Fargo & Co
- Store capital corporation
- Netflix Com Inc
- Bank of America
- Salesforce. Com Inc
- JP Morgan Chase & Co
- Berkshire Hathway Inc
- GW Pharmaceuticals
- Spotify Technology
- Oracle Corporation
- Cannabics Pharmaceuticals Inc
- Adobe Systems Inc

- Abbive Inc
- MasterCard Incorporated
- AXIM Biotechnologies Inc
- PayPal Holding Inc
- Microsoft Corp

So I just listed over 50+ stock investments for you to get into. These won't make you "filthy rich", however these are investments that pay you out in dividends and your money compounds over time. These are long term low risk and conservative investments.

There is always risk involved in investing, but the listed stocks I have given you are unlikely to fault, but will always have the possibly to lose value. Thus, again I suggest before putting any money into the mentioned stocks please do your due diligence.

I just gave you a guiding hand and direction of what to invest in. These are all corporations with intrinsic value derived from either a product or service they provide. Also, companies that have proven track records of success in bringing value to the marketplace by serving consumers.

Chapter 4: Real Estate

Earlier I discussed real estate being a true form of passive income and this holds to be true as the real estate market can be considered to be almost entirely indestructible. Why do I say that? People need places to live no matter what profession or where they are located, thus real estate can be thought of as guaranteed income for the person who owns the property.

For the purpose of this chapter and book I will only be covering American real estate.

There's a lot of misconceptions out there and in this chapter I will uncover the truth and fundamentals you will need to learn in order to get into real estate. This chapter is not a substitute for any real estate courses, but this is more of a general summary to get your feet wet and give you an idea of how things work in this industry.

There's a reason why the rich play the game of real estate, well there's actually multiple reasons, but here are the main ones; high ticket, good cash flow and its passive income.

High ticket – this simply means the transaction value is extraordinarily high. A real estate agent makes his/her commissions off a percentage of the unit sold. So for example, if you are a intermediate real estate agent and let's say you are getting a 4% commission on a $500,000 property, once you successfully close the deal your cashing in $**20,000 dollars USD**! (0.004 x 500,000) You can see why real estate is such an attractive prospect and lucrative endeavor. And if you are the property owner your looking to make a continuous monthly cashflow of a few thousand per month and if people are renting you can easily raise prices according to the market value.

However, its not as easy as many make out to be. There's quite the extensive process which includes phones calls back and forth between agents, client and property owner meetings, lawyers are involved, property inspectors, pest inspectors, insurance, credit checks, closing costs, signing papers, mortgages, opening and funding in escrow. As you can see this is quite the extensive process and in reality before you even get your cheque you'd be surprised at the amount of hands taking from your earnings before you even get your payment!

Cashflow - Real estate is a great cashflow vehicle whether you are a real estate agent or property owner. Long wait times and huge payouts is what constitutes the realm of real estate on both sides of the spectrum. Single units are not necessarily the best investment vehicle for your real estate portfolio, I would recommend going for apartment complexes, duplexes, triplexes, quadplex etc. The more units the better.

Why you may ask? Well, imagine the kind of cash flow that comes from multiple units, thinking about it 5 units vs 1 unit? Cleary 5 units is a more favorable cashflow situation as oppose to owning only one property. Cost of living is always on the rise, hence rent prices are subject to change according to market value meaning increased cashflow for you too. – Another reason to own multiple units!

Passive Income – The allure of passive income has captivated many, but only a few achieve this form of income through investing in certain vehicle or assets producing positive recurring cashflow on a monthly basis. Passive income is the dream of many, being able to have your money work for you in a systemic method where you are just collecting cheques on a monthly basis, sounds like the next best thing to winning the lottery right?

But, as mentioned earlier don't let passive income create a state of complacency in your life where you don't pay attention to your income and it eventually disappears. Real estate is an incredible passive income vehicle and is one of the most secure if not the most secure form of passive income. How? As mentioned earlier people will ALWAYS need a place to live, and thus you owning properties puts you at an advantage. Not even new technological advancements can disrupt real estate! – Its almost indestructible, the only exception is natural disasters. For the sake of this chapter we will discuss the two types of people who provide you this rental income. The two types of people are either private or subsidized tenants by government, I personally prefer private tenants I don't like dealing with section 8 subsidized funding from the government.

Although it can be considered a more secure form of income as it comes from governments, but you are in for inherent delays of long periods of wait times and you deal with a less than ideal demographic who can cause you trouble down the road. Not only that, but to continue to upkeep government subsidy you have to meet a criteria and ongoing inspections which is a hassle to deal with.

The best way to go about renting out your properties is through comprehensive credit checks and background checks of your potential candidate that is preferably a private tenant.

Passive income enables you to live the life you always wanted. You can leverage the nature of this type of income and participate in other business endeavors, spend more time with your family, more leisure time, vacation, etc. It comes with a lot of perks, but does take a lot of work to setup to get it right. Its not an overnight get rich quick scheme, but is a long term investment for the business savvy.

My advice is start with online business or stocks and get your first-hand experiences with passive income and than when your comfortable move on to more higher ticket items like real estate.

How To Find Real Estate Deals

The first thing you want to do is look up property management firms who have properties and request for vacant properties in a desired zip code (where you live) and this could mean single family homes, apartments units, condos, townhouses duplexes, quadplexes , etc.

What if I'm still having trouble find deals? What you can try is sending out flyers to owners who have what is known as "free and clear properties" meaning they have full ownership and there is no legal or financial restraints. These types of owners are most likely fall into the older/senior demographic of society. – This strategy is known as owner financing.

So how do you pitch to them? They may think of the following when you approach them "why would they finance to you and have the note on it when they can easily become the lender to you and accumulate interest from your payments just like the banks?"

This is what you would advise them that the fact that their property which has been owned for over 25+ years has fully depreciated and this means major tax benefits are lost, thus there left with a few options. – Doing a 10-

31 exchange means they would have to buy another piece of real estate and potentially get another mortgage, and they would not want to do this. You will advise them that if they do sell to you they don't have to do a 10-31 property exchange, taxes on capital gains will be done in installments over time and not all at once, and this means they get to spread their tax liabilities, and have more cash flow.

So if you are having trouble finding deals go the "free and clear" property route, write letters , send emails or flyers to your intended recipients.

The next way to find lucrative real estate deals if your still having trouble is to look into buying equity instead of cashflow deals. Now I know this may seem controversial, but just take a moment to listen, find a house that needs some repairs or is not in the best shape, add in some repairs and renovations and you have just increased the equity on your property. Let's say you bought a property worth 400k and renovated the entire kitchen for 5k, but added to its equity and increased the property value to 500k, you just made a 95k profit if you were to go this route and flip it. Remember ensure it's a cosmetic fix and not a structural fix.

Again, this in all honesty is not my preferred method, but just another strategy you can look at if your having trouble finding deals. I will admit cashflow is king, and in this kind of deal there really is no cashflow your taking a gamble at investing into the house's equity and in hopes to flip it for a tidy profit.

Now that I've discussed other methods of finding real estate deals I also want to discuss things you shouldn't do. Do not lower the quality standard of your real estate, meaning don't cheap out on upgrades, renovations and certainly do not buy poorly designed architecture or any buildings that have not been properly structurally maintained. As mentioned previously if your going to attempt to flip make sure it's a cosmetic fix and not a structural fix! – Structural fixes are extremely expensive.

My next piece of advise if your not experienced and new to real estate is don't buy outside of your living parameters. Why do I say this? Well, as soon as you move out of your familiar zone by default your most likely now facing uncharted territory outside your realm of expertise. (out of area means 40 mins away)

Think about it you decide to buy a unit on a street that you initially thought was a steal, but little did you know that particular area has higher crime rates and lower re-sell value. You wouldn't believe how often this happens to people who think they're getting a quick fixer upper to make a tidy profit, but in reality are actually getting the shorter end of the stick.

If your just starting out in real estate I highly recommend you start small and work your way up. Simplicity is the way to go, and don't get locked into something that's more than you can handle. Invest for the long term, and always do your due diligence. Starting out I also highly suggest you use real estate agents and perhaps even hire property managers if you can afford to.

My Recommended Top Property Management Companies:

Arizona

Saving Grace Investments, Glendale

Real Property Management Titanium, Tucson

Gorenter, Phoenix

California

Blackstone Realty & Management, Beverly Hills

West Point Property Management, Huntington Beach

Real Property Management San Diego Shores, San Diego

Colorado

Denver Property Management & Leasing, Centennial

Renters Warehouse Denver, Westminster

Echo Summit 16 Touch Management, Greenwood Village

Florida

Exit Realty Professionals Elite, Clermont

All County Elite Property Management, West Palm Beach

Florida Coastal Property Management, Jacksonville Beach

Georgia

Meridian Management Group, Atlanta

Myers Team Realty, Loganville

Solutions Realty Network, Tyrone

Illinois

Prestige Management Solutions, Arlington Heights

Real Property Management Group, Chicago

Grid 7 Properties, West Dundee

Maryland

REMAX American Dream, Baltimore

Reside Real Estate & Property Management, Lanham

Coakley Realty Management, Rockville

Michigan

Mutual Property Management, Farmington

East Side Property Services, Rochester

North Bloomfield Properties, West Bloomfield

Minnesota

Northpoint Asset Management MN, Edina

R.E.I. Property Management, Minneapolis

Realty Connect, Shakopee

Missouri

Oz Accommodations, Cass County

Elite Property Management, St. Charles

Pyramid Realty Group, St. Louis

North Carolina

Northpoint Asset Management NC, Charlotte

APS Realty Group, Clemmons

Alarca Property Management, Mooresville

New Jersey

Abacus Avenue Property Management, Hoboken

Craig Raymond Properties, Marlton

T.R.M. Property Management, Trenton

Nevada

PMI Las Vegas, Las Vegas

RE/MAX Affiliates Property Management, Henderson

Simply Property Management-Paielli Realty, Las Vegas

New York

Real Property Management New York Gold, Queens

NYC Apartment Management, Manhattan

Tristate Property Management Services, New York City

Ohio

RE/MAX Edge Realty, Canton

Property Management Pros, Columbus

Gem City Property Management, Dayton

Pennsylvania

Del Val Property Management, Malvern

Atlas Property Management, Philadelphia

Onyx Management Group, Southampton

Texas

Real Property Management LoneStar, Austin

Northpoint Asset Management Dallas, Fort Worth

Rave Property Management, Round Rock

Utah

Real Property Management Elite, West Jordan

Premier Real Estate Services, Salt Lake City

Elite Realty Management, Sandy

Virginia

Patriot Properties, Leesburg

The Wright Choice Richmond Realty Group, Richmond

The Kris Weaver Real Estate Team, Virginia Beach

Washington

Real Property Management of N. Puget Sound, Everett

MacPhersons Property Management, Shoreline

Brink Property Management, Seattle/Bellevue

No Money Down Real Estate?

You've probably heard this term before, "no money down real estate", and most of you wanting to get into real estate are probably wondering how on earth do you get enough money to even start this venture?

First off we must establish there are a few categories to real estate investing and they are as follow Wholesaling, Fixing and flipping houses, and multiple smaller income properties. Let's dissect each category so you have a more comprehensive understanding.

What is wholesaling exactly? This is simply when a property under contract for sale is at a very favorable discount and sells to a cash buyer who is offering to pay more than you have agreed to pay. This happens in one of the two ways, either by assigning the purchase agreement or do what is called a double closing.

Assigning the purchase agreement - In order to execute this strategy you will need a list of leads of eager sellers. Once you found your ideal list of sellers you will need to send out postcards or flyers stating the following " sell your property for instant cash in as little as 3-days. Avoid paying miscellaneous expenses and real estate commissions. You can sell in current condition, no repairs necessary under reasonable circumstances".

The key here to captivate this demographic of sellers is to mention you can sell the "property in its current condition". I will give you an example of a property I purchased using the assigning purchase agreement method.

After I distributed my post-card with my sales pitch I mentioned earlier I received a call within a few days from a prospect willing to sell to me! This property owner had amassed quite the extensive and impressive real estate portfolio. The thing was this particular property a single detached house was not in the best condition. So he asked me to give him an offer. This property had a market value of $**75,000.**

I did my research of the area and real estate market. I offered to pay **$37,000** and the owner had some time to sit and think about it, and later agreed to my offer under the condition if he could sell it to me in its current condition.

So remember I don't have the cash to dish out to pay the **$37,000** , and thus I start advertising on kijji ,craigslist or any other online marketing platform you can think of. I list the property for sale for **$45,000** a limited time offer.

A real estate investor called me and agreed to take me on my offer of **$45,000.** Hence, I just made a profit from the difference of **_45,000-37,000 = $8,000 profit._** You see the beauty in this method is I didn't even need cash to start out with! -This 100% no money down and all I did was facilitate the transaction process by being the middleman. No credit cards or lines of credits were used. 0% money down from my end. Remember these are deals you have to search for and hustle for as they're not just going to fall from the sky and into your lap.

I'll go over the gist of this case study again just in case you may be confused or missed anything. This is a no money down deal:

1. Property is valued at $75,000

2. My offer is accepted for $37,000

3. I list the same property for sale for $45,000

4. I profit $8,000 from this deal when someone accepts my offer($45,000-37,000= profit 8,000)

Essentially I find a property that I can flip it and make an offer for an under market value price point and than take that same property and list it for a higher price point that I can make a profit off. You assign your rights (using assignment purchase and sales agreement document) from the purchasing sales agreement that will transfer over to the cash buyer, so remember your agreeing to buy the property from the owner for $37,000 and the cash buyer is agreeing to purchase from you at $45,000, and you make a profit from the difference ($8,000).

Double closing – The second method mentioned in this chapter is known as double closing and this methodology tends to even be more lucrative in wholesaling. Remember in this method your actually selling your "contract" and not the house.

A = Property Owner selling property ***200k***

B= You

C= Investor/Cash Buyer ***250k***

So how does this methodology work? (A) uses purchase sales agreement document with (B), than you advise (A) you will have the cheque for them the following day and you both will have to designate a title company/ attorney's office to conduct this in. At this point you will create another purchase sales agreement document, but this time between (B)-(C), and the key to how this method works is everything happens in "escrow".

Here's what happens you (B) will give (A) property seller what is called earnest money and this payment is a specific form of security deposit that confirms you have the intention to purchase the property. Earnest money is a nominal fee, for this example well say it's a $100. So at this point you deposit $100 into escrow, and now you record the deed.

On transaction day (C) the investor who is paying cash will wire money to (B) you, remember this will only work for full cash payments, no bank loans. You are flipping the property, thus you are selling for 250k. You are wired the 250k from the cash buyer, and than you take that same money and fully close (A)-(B) by purchasing the property. The property owner will receive 200k the value he is selling the property for, and you will pocket 50k. – Remember there are closing costs between 2.5%-3% and this will come out of 50k you profited.

At this point both parties are satisfied you closed both (A)-(B) and (B)-(C) with two separate sales agreement documents. I prefer to close (B)-(C) first before closing (A)-(B) due to the fact the property owner may potentially cause issues if he/she doesn't receive the money right away.

Remember this form of wholesaling is all done in escrow. You are using the cash buyer's funds to pay for the entire transaction.

I will reiterate the process below one more time in this double closing deal step by step.

A = Property Owner selling property ***200k***

B= You

C= Investor/Cash Buyer ***250k***

1. (A)-(B) purchase sales agreement is signed. You deposit "earnest money" ($100) in escrow.
2. (B)-(C) purchase agreement is signed. You are wired the full cash amount of 250k in escrow.
3. You now take that 250k and close A-B for 200k and receive ownership of the property (deed).
4. You now take that deed and fully close B-C by depositing the deed to the cash buyer.
5. Both purchase sales agreements are successfully closed and you pocketed approximately **50k** - minus any closing costs.

This is the other way which I prefer doing double closing starting from B-C, see below..

A = Property Owner selling property **200k**

B= You

C= Investor/Cash Buyer **250k**

1. (B)-(C) purchase agreement is signed. You are wired the full cash amount of 250k in escrow.
2. You now take that 250k and close (A)-(B) for 200k and receive ownership of the property (deed).
3. You now take that deed and fully close B-C by depositing the deed to the cash buyer.
4. Both purchase sales agreements are successfully executed and you pocketed approximately **50k** - minus any closing costs.

That is the gist of wholesaling and buying property with little to no money down. Go over it a few times and familiarize yourself with the process it maybe a little confusing at first, but once you understand the fundamentals you should be able to grasp the concept fully.

I would also like to note there is an element of confidentiality in case your wondering. The title company/attorney's office orchestrating the procedure will keep things confidential as you don't want to affect working relations between you and the property seller if they find out how much your pocketing. Some property sellers may want to re-negotiate or dispute the deal if they find out how much your profiting, thus the importance of confidentiality in the nature of this transaction.

So to summarize this no money down..

1. Find eager sellers with robust portfolios and strong equity/ (using flyers/post cards/ emails)
2. Control the property
3. Choose either to flip the agreement or double close

Apartment Building Investing

In this section I will cover investing in real estate with under performing apartment buildings and teach you how to leverage them for more positive cashflow and ultimately financial stability or freedom.

Investing in apartment complexes or even duplexes, triplexes and quadplexes is more lucrative than investing in single family home properties. Why? The simple reason is cashflow! Especially, with apartment complexes your positive cashflow is very favorable, imagine a 25 unit apartment complex and even if its not at full capacity you still make a great cashflow. Imagine only 12 tenants are renting out of the 25 units, and rent is between $900-$1200 per month, you can imagine the type of cashflow your receiving on a monthly basis as oppose to one pillar of income from a single family home.

Before buying your first apartment unit its obvious you need a team of skilled individuals inspectors, lawyers, and possibly real estate agents. I want to highlight the importance of having phenomenal inspectors for your apartment units and not to cheap out on them! An inspector can make or break you. Why are they so important? Well, you want your inspector going through every single unit within your apartment complex taking pictures, documenting and recording problems such as broken glass, leaks, infrastructure issues, etc.

A picture is worth a thousand words and having these reports from your inspector can give you an idea of projecting potential costs for fixing up the property. – Note, if you do run into serious structural issues, I strongly suggest you do NOT buy the property as structural issues are very expensive. If your looking for a fixer upper you need to aim for cosmetic level issues not structural problems.

So what do you do when you discover that there is in fact a problem with a apartment complex your interested in purchasing? You will have to do something called a "repair allowance" during the closing of the deal and what this entails is you tell the seller you want a repair allowance, thus you will raise the value of the property to a certain amount and be credited that back after closing. So for instance, your purchasing an apartment complex at 900k, but you request for repair allowances to be including causing the selling price to rise to 920k. Hence, the seller will still receive his/her 900k, but you will be credited the 20k after the deal is closed.

Get To Know Your Properties

(A) Properties - "A listed" properties are higher end and I strongly suggest you stay away from these types. These properties are usually for the elite and rich who have nothing better to do with their money and thus they just blow it on a very expensive real estate property. For instance, like a luxury multimillion dollar mansion used as a rental. The cashflow on that is terrible as you don't have a large consumer base who can afford that, and the maintenance and upkeeping cost are through the roof and most likely will cause you to be in the red. There is very little cashflow on these types of properties let alone creational wealth, its more or less an attempt to maintain wealth as oppose to wealth creation.

(B) properties- B listed properties tend to be in the range of 30 to up to 50 years old. These are the type of properties and real estate deals you want to look for. Combination of blue collar and white collar tenants, and this is what you want the tenant base to be for consistent positive recurring cashflow on a monthly basis. These properties are a little old and may need some level of maintenance and upkeeping time to time.

(C) properties – C listed properties are usually overlooked that have a lot of cosmetic issues going on with them. But, they do cashflow very nicely just like (B) listed properties. A key way to leverage C properties is if you have a C listed property in a predominantly (B) property area you've just struck gold because you can easily reposition the C property by adding upgrades and fixing any cosmetic issues and have it serve in the (B) property market. C properties are one of the best cashflow vehicles if you know what you are doing and know what to look for. – Properties with only cosmetic issues, but located in a favorable area. After you get the hang of this you can also start doing something called a "10-31" exchange which is a trade up for property, reinvesting your proceeds from selling the C property to acquire (B) properties, and as an added bonus you defer paying capital gains tax!

(D) properties – To put it bluntly these are "ghetto" properties high maintenance and very management intensive. Involved with government section 8 and government housing aspect of real estate, rough neighborhoods and can get dangerous. A lot of lenders and even banks are unlikely to approve loans for these

types of properties. I would suggest you stay away and refrain from investing in this type of real estate. Not only is it management intensive, but will require a lot of "waiting" for payments as these are not quality tenants. One of the few benefits is that government pays between 70-80% and sometimes even 100% of tenants costs for rent, but that means your in for extended wait times that can be infuriating. Longer than normal wait times will effect your cashflow.

Not a real estate investment I favor although there are people making good money with this type of investment, but I am certainly not a fan and wouldn't recommend it. Also, sometimes you are only paid cash only for rent so again this posses a safety risk for you. There's a lot of turn over, constant renovations and upgrades, etc. You may have tenants in at full capacity, but what does that benefit you if you cannot collect rent? Tenants can also be delinquents when they get their cheques from the government and not spend it on rent. This leaves you with little choice, but to follow a long procedure for the eviction process. -There is just to much hassle for (D) class properties.

Benefits of Multiple Units VS Single Family Homes

Not only from a cashflow perspective is having a multiple unit complex far superior than a single family home, but its easier to manage as oppose to having multiple single family homes. Think about it all your tenants are found in one central location whether it's an apartment, duplex, triplex or quadplex, and rent is collected in one location. One boiler, roof, and lawn. If you were to go the route of multiple single family units you would have a nightmare of a time trying to manage tenants, maintenance and everything is just spread out which is inconvenient.

Grasping The Real Estate Market

Whether you are a first time home buyer, real estate investor, house flipper, wholesaler or simply want to learn the ins and outs of the real estate market this section will cover the fundamentals you will need to understand before getting your feet wet in real estate.

There are two layers or levels to real estate the macro level that encompasses the entire market and the local level which is usually within your social surrounds. The macro level of real estate is complex and can be difficult to understand and predict fluctuations or declines. But at the local level you can more easily grasp things with more certainty.

There are various factors to look at before purchasing real estate as the property's value is actually derived from its surroundings! – And not necessarily entirely the property itself. These are fundamentals factors to look for when looking to buy real estate, and if you do not see these elements in play than I would suggest to refrain from getting into that particular segment of real estate.

*A well known fact is that optimal location is key to a successful real estate investment. Let's take a deeper look at what location encompasses in the following.

Factors that Influence The Value of Real Estate

Schools

Malls/Supermarkets

Employment

Recreation Centres

Beaches/ Parks

Bus Terminals

Crime Rates

Population Density

Price Range

Schools- There is a strong correlation between real estate and the geographical location of schools. This could mean either elementary school, high school and universities. These institutions dictate a lot of real estate deals whether people are investors, flippers, wholesalers or home buyers. Ideally people want to live in relatively close proximity to where a school is to cut down on commute times.

Especially with university students who rent, -the market is hot when you have a university within close proximity of your real estate investment. The cashflow is very strong in an investment that relies on students as the supply of student continues to increase every year for students who move out to study and have their "college experience", and this also includes international students as well.

Malls/Supermarket - Another cornerstone to selecting a good real estate property is malls/supermarkets. Let's face it people want to be able to buy food, groceries, and clothing somewhere that is accessible to where they live. Hence, the importance of doing your research on the location of malls/supermarkets as this will heavily dictate whether people will buy property or not. – Nobody wants to live in the middle of nowhere and go out of their way to travel to the store.

Employment – This is a very under looked facet to real estate. So what is the importance of employment rate? Employment is quintessential to real estate because people need money to pay for rent! – Which equates to your cashflow.

This means if there are no good job prospects or under performing employment opportunities this could affect your cashflow and quality of tenants. The last thing you want is a bad tenant who has trouble paying rent and having to go through the whole eviction process! Especially in some states, like California where it seems the tenants rights to live in your property appears to be favored over your own right as a property owner.

Ergo, the importance of screening your tenants thoroughly by doing a little digging on their background, employment, and especially their credit! If in your search you discover any red flags at any of the above mentioned aspects I would strongly recommend you do not give them the opportunity to be your tenant. A bad tenant can be costly and could ruin your real estate investment, and just turn things into a nightmare for you.

Part of my process of screening my tenants is there job occupation and retention. By finding out what they do for a living you can gauge the kind of money they bring in and this should give you an idea if they can afford your rent. The next thing to look for is job retention rate which means if you find out they have had unstable employment, meaning cannot hold a job for less than 6 months this should also indicate a red flag to you and thus do not allow them residence. Think about it if they are constantly leaving their jobs for whatever reason it could be health related or perhaps there just bad employees you do not want to be stuck with the short end of the stick when rent time comes around because they'll be short on cash.

Another known fact is people tend to live where there job is for the most part. When I use to work as a concierge at an apartment complex that was near a hospital which was across the street literally and near other business office towers, I can't emphasize enough how much people resided within this apartment complex simply because it was near where they worked. This place had lawyers, doctors, nurses, researchers, accountants etc, and anytime I would converse with them they complained about certain things in regards to the apartment amenities and flaws, but would always note they choose to "live here because its close to where they work", although they can afford a much nicer place to reside.

Case in point the importance of employment rates, opportunities and job prospects within real estate.

Things to look for in regards to employment prospects which can dictate your success? Oil sands, tech start ups, hospitals, law firms, business office towers, automotive plants, etc. There is indeed a strong correlation between booming real estate and place of employment.

Now let's look at the other side of the spectrum, massive lay offs, job cuts, outsourcing and factories closing down. This would indicate a bad real estate investment due to the fact that employment opportunities are severely lacking. So how do we access this pertinent information?

You can access information on employment rates by going to the local employment office or search online for your local area. Another strategy to find out employment rates is old fashion, but extremely effective, and that's observing your surroundings; are there any new developments for job opportunities within the area? Car factories, restaurants, malls, etc.

Recreation Centres- Facilities such as recreation centres are also influential variables when it comes to buying your real estate. What will your tenant do in their leisure time? Recreation centres are crucial in regards to leisure activities, and this could be summer camp for kids, sports, entertainment, volunteering, etc. Whatever the case may be finding real estate near recreation centres would also be a good idea to enhance your real estate investment potential.

Beaches/ Parks- Beaches and parks although not essential could be the difference between you making a small amount of income versus huge monthly cashflow payouts. What do I mean by this? Beaches or parks function like a aesthetic landmark and add a certain appealing decorative touch to your real estate investment. The fact is real estate found within the proximity or located directly near parks or beaches are astronomically higher in price range compared to regular real estate that does not have beaches or parks.

Meaning you can charge higher premiums for properties located by the beach/park. People want to live by nature and view its beauty, and on top of that go to the beach for some summer time fun. These types of real estate deals are gems and can be extremely lucrative investments for you. People are willing to pay the higher rates for this type of real estate as it appeals to them.

Bus Terminals (transportation) - Bus terminals are also central tenets to the success of your real estate investment. Let's face it not everybody drives to work or for that matter drives at all. People need transportation regardless, so places where there is accessible and easy subway access is crucial to your real estate. You can easily use google maps to research this factor before choosing a real estate property.

People need this type of transportation to get to work, beat traffic, travel, etc. You can kind of see how there is an overlap to a lot of these mentioned factors. Schools are usually located near the proximity of bus terminals, and malls are usually located where there is a high population of kids. You can see this almost symbiotic relationship between schools, transportation and real estate. People need places to live, but than they need school for their kids, and these kids need transportation, and malls leverage off both the need for transpiration and the traffic of consumers who will spend money which can be kids or adults.

Identifying these kinds of patterns are crucial to the success of your real estate. Did you know the success of **McDonalds** really has nothing to do with how well they make burgers or even marketing? But the strategic location of real estate is what matters! – How's that for some food for thought?

Crime Rates – A more sobering aspect to real estate and reality. Crime heavily influences where people will decide to live, and if there is a lot of "street activity", gangs, drugs, extortion, break and enters, etc your real estate can depreciate in value very quickly. I had an inexperienced friend who decided to buy real estate outside of his living parameters and I mentioned earlier you should NOT go outside of 40 mins from where you live, especially if you are inexperienced to the real estate game.

Guess what happened? He thought he found an incredible deal just a few blocks away from a hot market.

Literally a few blocks down the street from the hot real estate where it was booming, he found pockets of area that had very cheap properties. My friend decided to buy a property, but little did he know about the crime rate. So what happened?

After purchasing the property my friend had trouble finding tenants to rent too and on top of that had a few break and enters because certain unscrupulous individuals noticed that this property was vacant for quite some time. He was later forced to sell the property at a loss, and never made his ROI. Again, the reality of crime rates must be recognized and you must become self-aware of your surroundings. To find out crime rates just do a simple google search of " how to find crime rates in your area/neighborhood", this should be able to provide you the necessary tools for this task.

Population Density – Another variable to factor in to the success or failure of your real estate is dependent on population density. This also ties into supply of property, but what exactly is population density? This is simply the measure of population per unit or area by volume. So how does this and supply of property relate to your real estate investment? Well, you want to ensure that there is no shortage of properties and a steady supply, but also on the other end of the spectrum you want to focus on how much of the populace are actually tenants within the area.

If there are properties that are not being filled with tenants than you could have a serious problem, this would indicate there is no demand. So you want to be able to identify the volume of people living within a given area and if there is enough housing to accommodate them. I've been in towns where there are a flood of condos being built and going on the market, but there was no interest or demand meaning some of these projects flat out failed. The blame really goes to the property developers in these types of cases because they didn't do their due diligence and research on the real estate market. If there are no schools, malls, means of transportation, and aesthetic appeals such as parks or beaches, than chances are people would no want to live there. But on the flip side of things, if you have all the crucial elements that make real estate successful, but have high crime rate this could also disproportionally effect your real estate.

Price range – This may seem like the most obvious factor when it comes to real estate, but its not emphasized nearly enough. By price range I am referring to affordability. Can people afford to live at your real estate investment? The last thing you want is to buy a multi-million dollar investment property and pay extremely high maintenance fees only to find out that nobody can afford your property! There have been a number of accounts of people doing just that and this just means they failed to due their due diligence and research their demographics.

Ultimately, people want a place they can afford and neglecting this fact could be costly for you. So its up to you to figure out the local household income within your demographic of real estate. – You want to find the average or median household income people make within the parameters of your real estate investment. A google search of this can help you find out.

After you've figured the median house hold income you want to extrapolate that and find out how much of that amount of people who are willing to spend based on today's interest rates. You can call a mortgage broker to find out or use online tools to figure this out. Once you find out that maximum amount people are willing to spend on a property you than will find out the median house price within the area. Once you have these two figures you will want to see if in fact people' household income can actually afford the average house price.

Before starting any real estate investment select your asset class and pick the niche you want to specifically target. The biggest mistake I see novice real estate investors make is trying to chase after everything only to get nothing! You may be wondering why this might be a bad idea?

You probably think diversification is a key pillar to financial stability, and there is some truth to that, but when your starting out you should be "laser pin point focused". Meaning you select one niche or asset class whether that be flipping houses, wholesaling, investing in single family homes, duplexes, triplexes, quadplexes, apartment complexes, student homes, government housing, etc. You need to really stay focused on one dimension of real estate before you can branch out and diversify.

Because what happens when you have no initial goal? If you don't have a target how are you going to hit it? It doesn't make sense to expend your time , energy and hard earned dollars trying to chase every opportunity that comes your way, when you should actually be waiting for the right opportunity that meets your target goal.

5 Must Know Real Estate Tips

1. List on MLS – If your selling bottom line if your not listed on the MLS you are potentially losing out on big bucks. You don't get the full exposure your property deserves by not paying to be listed for MLS. When your in real estate you can't cheap out, and although Craigslist and other free methods may work, but just remember you lose out on full exposure on the marketplace and could lose out on a potential lucrative offer.

2. Get multiple bids - This is pretty straight forward, but I feel it needs to be addressed. You need get at least a minimum of 3 bids. -In essence this is a price match strategy by compare and contrast and is very effective. I'll explain, for instance if you need to get your roof replaced ask bids from 3 different roofers, if you have plumbing issues get 3 bids from 3 separate plumbers, air conditioning issues get 3 bids from different repair men, and if you need a mortgage get 3 bids from different mortgage brokers. – There is this misconception your credit being pulled more than once will hurt your credit score, which is not at all true! The fact is you can get as many soft credit pulls as you want within a **2 week period** and it won't hurt your credit at all! But they won't tell you that! This simple yet effect compare and contrast strategy will save you tons of money. Think about it if you get one offer why on earth would you blindly accept it without shopping around elsewhere? I bet you compare and contrast for smaller things, why not do this with real estate? Do your due diligence.

3. Strategic Price Point - The importance of pricing your property low must be emphasized because you can never price your property to low. Why you may ask? Well, because strategically pricing your property low relative to market prices will cause you to get multiple offers, and the people bidding will bid the property back up to what the market value actually is. Do you see how beautifully that works when orchestrated

correctly? You lure offers in with a low price point, but the multiple offer situation causes an increase in price and your property will bounce back up to its market value. On the opposite end of the spectrum if you list too high you are actually doing yourself a disservice because nobody will purchase it and it will sit stale on the market creating an impression that something could be potentially wrong with your property.

4. Be Skeptical - My 4th point might have you wondering what do you mean be skeptical? I'll explain, you see both sellers and buyers are liars! You must verify all claims from either buyers and sellers, do not take their word for it no matter how charming they may appear to be. Do your due diligence and double check. For instance, if someone is selling you a property and they say the house is in perfect condition and nothing has ever happened. -Make sure you verify by hiring the best inspector you can to ensure if in fact the house is in good condition. I had a situation like this before where a seller was pitching me the house was pristine and unscathed. I sent my

inspector in and guess what I found out? The basement had some serious structural damages from flooding and the attic had fire damage! You should of seen the reaction of the seller's face when I told him of my discovery. The last thing you want is to get the short end of the stick, so always verify! The same goes for a buyer, when they say they got the cash, credit, loan, proof of approval for funds, line of credits etc, do your due diligence call the mortgage broker and ask if that person is qualified to buy your property.

5. Patience – The old adage is true patience is a virtue and ever more so important in the realm of real estate. Real estate can either be your biggest mistake or biggest success story depending on how you execute. Make sure you have clear intentions and solid contingency plans in place because the last thing you want to do is buy a piece of property and be stuck with it for the rest of your life. There are huge risks to real estate and once you commit to a home and if you made your purchase in haste you can think of that home as your jail! There are so many new homeowners who got into real estate very easily, but are having an extremely difficult time to sell. Avoid emotional decisions and attachments to any and all properties, and buy according to the

facts at hand. Sometimes the best move is not to make a move at all, thus refraining from committing to a deal you can't hold down. Better to refrain and defer your emotions than have regret for the rest of your life.

Bonus Tip- Minimalist living. Buy less than you can afford because when you get a new house you have a whole range of expenses coming your way you never expected. You could face piping problems, air conditioning issues, roof replacement and leaking, etc. Hence, the importance of living below your means so you have a good financial cushion to fall back on.

Rental VS Flipping Property

To be quite honest whether getting into rentals or flipping properties as an investment vehicle is right for you will be dependent on your financial goals and your situation. Both these real estate endeavors can be extremely lucrative when done right, however based on your personalize situation you may lean towards one or the other.

Before looking at anything you must consider the following, risk involved, money required, return rate on investment and the amount of time you will have to spend. So lets take a look at rentals first.

<u>Rental Property Factors</u>

>**Risk** - Rentals generally speaking are less risky than flipping properties simply because you have tenants paying you every month and thus you have recurring cashflow on a monthly basis. Therefore, your able to pay down your mortgage and have a certain amount of profit.

Return - The return on your rental property should be anywhere between 12-20% which is a decent amount.

Required Money - Rental properties will require either on hand cash or credit from the bank, and you can even uses family or friends as investors too. Almost always a large amount of money is necessary to make the purchase for the property and depending on what property you selected you can make a good living off your rental. I recommend doing apartment units or at the least triplexes or quadplexes. Single family homes will not get you the cash necessary for real wealth creation, unless you have multiple single family homes.

Time Required - rentals don't actually require a lot of your time. You usually hire people to work for you whether that be realtors, contractors, and even property managers if necessary. Your probably looking around 5-10 hours of your time every month.

Flipping Property Factors

Risk- Flipping houses have more risks that come with it as you don't have tenants in place providing you that steady cashflow to help pay off your loan. Your aim is to buy properties that are overlooked on the market and only need cosmetic fixes and surface level patch ups. You do not want to buy a property with foundational or structural issues as this can be extremely costly and will eat away at your end profits. An inspector is essential for catching these things before you even make the purchase, hence hire the best inspector you can.

Return - With more risk comes a greater reward. Flipping properties can garner you a higher rate of return compared to rentals. On average flipping houses should only take you between 4-6 months, and you should be looking to make profits upwards of 30-50% profit!

Money Required - Flipping can be done without any money at all! That's right as earlier discussed in this chapter there are methods you can use to do "no money" down deals. Not only that but you can more easily find investors willing to fund your "fix and flip project" as oppose to a rental property because investors know a lot of money can be made off a flip.

Time Required - Flipping unlike rental properties will require you much more time. From managing and checking up on your contractors, listing the property on the open market (MLS), negotiating deals with various buyers and realtors, marketing and analyzing your bids.

How To Find Investors

Let's face it real estate requires a large amount of start up capital and the average person doesn't have hundreds of thousands of dollars saved up in their bank accounts. -Unless you inherited a fortune or won the lottery. But, if your like me when I started out you probably don't have the money to dish out.

Well, that's perfectly alright because that is where investors come into play. You see in real estate we use investors to fund either a portion or all of the capital needed for a real estate venture. Finding investors is a lot easier than you think, but its actually convincing investors to invest with you that is the difficult part. Can you blame them? Investors are very prudent with their money and don't want to take on any unnecessary risks that can cause them potential losses.

So how do we go about acquiring investors? Investors can be found at foreclosure offices making bids, seminars, real estate meet ups, and some may even be your friends or family. You must posses the knowledge, confidence and aptitude demonstrating your competence when conversating with your potential investor. Dress the part preferably business attire, people will judge you based on what you wear, drive, and your overall demeanor.

You must convince the investor your are the right person to manage their money. Your going to have to continuously educate yourself on real estate by reading at least 10 books on the topic, attend seminars and meet ups, and listen to more podcasts.

Once you can talk the lingo and have established rapport, building trust and securing their approval, only than will they be willing to invest with you. What value do you bring to the table? Can you bring a fresh perspective? The law of reciprocity is at play here, you must add value and in exchange they will give money to fund your project. If you can showcase to your potential investor you have an extensive knowledge base without condescending him, and even better educate him on something he doesn't already know. This leaves a strong and lasting impression that your someone who means business and you only need the funds to execute a deal.

I should also note the deal must be favorable to the investor as you can't give him the short end of the stick, and expect yourself to only walk away with a big chunk of the profit. If you need to make a little sacrifice and cut your profits by a little to make the deal more appealing, than I highly recommend you do so. If you can show that your willing to add value to their life, investors will be more inclined to invest with you.

You must have a deal under contract ready before you even think about approaching an investor. The last thing an investor wants is someone wasting their time speculating about a deal they don't have ready to go. This means you will first have to approach sellers and negotiate a deal with them before you go to a potential investor.

Different Type of Investors:

Hard Money Lenders – These investors interest rates are extremely high, unlike the bank who typically charges 3-5% for a mortgage hard money lenders charge upwards to 12% or more annually. Not only that but they also have up front costs they call "points" which is either 2 – 4 points up front. Meaning let's say you ask for a ten thousands dollar loan, they could very well ask you to pay them $2,000 -$4,000 dollars up front. This is just there way of ensuring they can hold some money as security and shows if your serious. This means your paying up front payments between $2000-$4000 + 12% annually.

This probably sounds absurd to you when compared to banks that can give you mortgages as low as 3-5%. The typical house for 100k your paying between $300-$500 per month using a bank mortgage, while hard money lenders would charge $1200+ per month! So why on earth would you eve accept a deal like this from hard money lenders? Well, you see hard money lenders approve loans only if you have a deal in place. They don't care about your credit score or any of that stuff at all.

Private Money Investors - These types of investors are more rare and favorable. They tend to have a lot of cash on hand, but don't charge extremely high interest rates like hard money lenders. Most of the time these types of lenders are willing to dish out 100% of the purchase price!

Smaller Investors – These constitute your friends, family and associates.

Whichever investor you select you will have to follow these fundamental principles before even approaching an investor, educating yourself on real estate, networking, adding value to people, and looking for the right deals.

Renting VS Owning

If your reading this book you probably want to sharpen your financial intelligence. Throughout this particular chapter I have discussed many strategies for you to utilize such as no money down deals, apartment investing, looking at location dynamics, and finding your ideal investors. But in this section I want to talk about the pros and cons to renting versus owning your property.

Buying a property is a life altering decision you can make that can either build your wealth or could cause a series of unfortunate events. Let's look some of the benefits and drawbacks of renting vs owning

Renting Benefits

No mortgage

You can be approved even with bad credit

Low maintenance costs

Location mobility

No market risk

Some utility bills included

Financial stability

Renting Drawbacks

Rent can be higher than mortgages

No Equity

You don't own the property

You cannot change or modify interior or exterior to your preference

Rents are not fixed and can fluctuate at landlord's discretion

Property owner can sell and ask you to leave at any point in time

Owning Benefits

Built equity and you own an asset

You can make renovations and upgrades at any time

Benefit market appreciation

Use property as a rental for cashflow

<u>Owning Draw Backs</u>

Mortgage

Maintenance costs

Property taxes

Insurance

If market dives your equity will decline

You have to qualify with income/ credit

I have provided you both sides to the story. The question is which scenario benefits your personalized financial situation? That you will have to come to terms with and answer yourself as everyone's situation is unique. I am personally one to gravitate towards to renting where I live, and own my assets that generate me a monthly recurring cashflow. – That's my philosophy and way of living. It's up to you to decide how you want to live and how you will structure these things.

One of my biggest pieces of advise is don't make emotional decisions or get emotionally attached. If your reading this book I officially pronounce you an investor in training and you cannot make decisions based on personal preferences. Your buy decisions must be logical and backed up by facts and not how you feel.

When a typical investor buys a property he/she is looking at the facts and if the numbers add up. They look for a property that is undervalued, but overlooked in the marketplace. Also, something that is appealing to the average consumer and something they can afford. Never buy the "nicest" house in a neighborhood, but select the house that is overlooked and needs cosmetic touch ups. So, you can renovate it and bring it up to par.

Real Estate hack – Living Rent FREE

In this section I am going to teach you a real estate strategy that can essentially give you rent free living! So how can this be done exactly? Well, first off you will need to look into purchasing multi-family property units which are duplexes, triplexes and even quadplexes. So the key here is if you acquire a quadplex for example you will rent out the 3 units and live in 1. Meaning the cashflow from all 3 units will be able to cover your mortgage on that property! There are so many benefits to this on top of living for free, for instance you can count the anticipated rental income as apart of your total annual income when qualifying for a bigger loans from the bank if you desire to buy more real estate.

So let me paint you a scenario to help you grasp the picture even better. Let's say you purchased the quadplex for $450,000, and your renting rate for the 3 units is $977 per month. If you put down 100k as a down payment your looking at a mortgage of around $1900 per month, property tax $400, and insurance $150.

So let's do the math if we add up all the property expenses we have around ***$2450*** per month and your monthly revenue from the quadplex is ***$2991***. So **$2991-$2450 = $541** net profit. So your living at your property for free, paying down your mortgage, property tax, insurance, and even have enough money left over for any unforeseen repairs or renovations, and pocketing $541 every single month! What an incredible hack living rent free and making a tidy profit, and best of all your tenants are paying your expenses every month! This is the ultimate house hack, and almost anyone has the capacity to pull it off assuming you can get approved for the loan. But it get's even better you can deduct one fourth of all the mortgage interest, property tax, and use any other expenses related to the property as a write off against the income you make. Hence, your income tax liability is dramatically decreased and you owe less to the IRS.

This was a general scenario I created, and obviously everyone's individual situation will vary case by case, but this is the gist of how to do a real estate hack by living rent free. Awesome cashflow, free rent, and you get to use your expenses you don't even pay for directly as write offs to lower the income tax you pay! – It doesn't get any better than this.

Now I'm not going to just paint you rainbows and roses. There are potential risks and downsides to this type of investment style. Since you'll be living where your tenants reside too there is a possibility you may develop close relationships and thus, tenants can take advantage of you when rent time comes around and skip out and make lame excuses and basically string you along. Hence, managing bad tenants could be a potential pitfall to this investment, but once you sift out all the bad ones and find your gems in the rough it'll be smooth sailing from there.

There will also be common areas you will be sharing and you may not be able to escape, thus giving you a lack of privacy. I have given both sides to this type of real estate investment and weighed the pros and cons. Its up to you to choose what your most comfortable in dealing with and remember to make an informed decision.

Property Management Advise

1. Always verify. Check credit reports, income statements, background checks, and anything else that may help you validate a tenant.

2. Don't get to close with your tenants. Developing relationships can be costly especially in business settings, and I see it happen all the time. The last thing you want is your tenants skipping out on rent and exploiting the friendship between you two to get away with not paying. Zero tolerance policy in effect and do not give into sob stories. Everybody has problems and your primary concern is to keep your property generating you positive cashflow recurring every month.

3. Co-occupation double verification. Imagine this scenario a couple is in a relationship one with good credit and another with bad credit decides to rent from you so they apply as "co-occupant", which is completely legal, however you must be proactive in this situation. What if the relationship falls apart and the occupant with

good credit decides to take off and your left with the tenant with bad credit? – Hence, its your responsibility to run a credit check on both occupants, and if either one has bad credit do not allow them residence.

4. Procedures when tenants gives you 30 day notice to vacate property? This is a crucial moment for you because you don't want to lose out on cashflow due to a vacant unit, thus your trying to fill the unit within 30 days with a new tenant, hence you will give your tenant a call and advise you will give a 24 hour notice for any new showings for new potential clients.

5. Before even giving your new tenant an application to apply do a comprehensive phone call interview initially. Hence, you can potentially save time before the actual in person screening of the tenant and get a feel of how they are like. – Do not use this phone call interview to replace the standard procedures from point # 1 I mentioned earlier.

Phone call interview questions: On what day do you plan to move in? How many occupants are moving in? Do you have any pets? Do you have allergies? What do you do for a living? What is your credit score? (tell them you are looking for tenants with scores of 700 and up)

6. Rent increase strategy- Never disclose you are the owner of the property. You take on the role of property manager, hence when you increase the rent after a certain time your tenant won't be angry directly towards you, but at the "owner". Remember you want your tenant happy and you want to build a good customer relation with them. If they know you're the owner there is more chances they will complain about every little thing and you won't hear the end of it. Hence you need to create the illusion of an anonymous owner.

Chapter 5: Business Fundamental Principles

Structuring Your Business The Right Way

In the section I will cover how to properly structure your business, guiding philosophies and principles to follow in order to achieve long term sustainable success. Business is ultimately about creating longevity that creates wealth and sustains itself, not a get rich quick scheme that only lasts a moment or an ephemeral experience.

In the last chapter I discussed real estate and taught you how to do no money down deals, how to find deals, investing in apartment complexes, what to look for and a whole bunch of other nuggets of knowledge. I wanted to touch a bit on structuring your business whether it be for real estate, online or retail business, and even stocks as this will be crucial in regards how much income you actually take away.

Business is not about how much you make, but how much you keep after taxes, expenses, payroll etc.

The first thing you must determine is whether you will be creating a LLC, S-corporation, C- Corporation, sole proprietorships, or limited liability partnerships. I strongly suggest you speak to a licensed chartered accountant so you can make an informed decision. They will go into in depth details with you on advantages and disadvantages that come with all these business structures.

I will touch on the fundamentals of a sole proprietorship, general partnerships and corporations.

Sole proprietorship – Is run by a single individual or married couple in one business. – In this type of business there is no legal distinction between you and the business, thus you are treated the same and if you were to get sued you are liable 100%. There really aren't any huge tax advantages apart from writing off business related expenses and being able to use that to offset the amount of income tax you pay on your net profits.

General Partnerships - Is basically the same as a sole proprietorship, but the only exception is you have partners who are equally liable for any litigation that may occur. Tax advantages are the same as a sole proprietorship.

Corporation - Considered legally an entity and comes with various taxation benefits. You will have board members whom you traditionally issue a certain number of shares of the company too, and these board members will have certain assigned functions and tasks to uphold that you the owner will dictate. The owner in most cases will own majority shares, and be considered majority shareholder which gives you authority over the company direction.

Tax advantages are favorable as you not only get to write business related expenses off to offset your corporate income tax, but you also get taxed at the corporate level which is much less than being taxed as an individual. For instance, if you make 100k a year as an individual a big junk of that around 35%-50% or even more will go to the tax man depending on which state you live in. That's state personal income tax for you, but on the other hand if you make 100k as a corporation you only pay between 15%-20% in taxes depending which state you live in. In some states such as Delaware you pay next to nothing in taxes, except nominal annual tax fees that is approximately $250.

Also there are tax mitigation strategies you can utilize like being paid in dividends which is also taxed at a much lower rate depending on which state you live in. Again, all these things you will need to discuss in further in depth detail with a licensed accountant.

As for legal ramifications you are more secure than sole proprietorships and general partnerships, however this doesn't mean you are completely 100% immune personally. Although creating a corporation by default gives you a lot of protection that other business structures cannot provide, but there are a few exceptions. Generally speaking, when a corporation is sued since it is considered a separate legal entity you are protected personally and the plaintiff cannot touch your personal assets he or she can only go after things under the corporate entity's name. But here's where things get interesting, if someone can prove that your corporation is nothing more than a mere shell company or a front that is just using a corporate structure as a pretext and has no genuine company operational activities. What this means is in theory they can pierce through your company and pursue you personally. This is called " piercing the corporate veil", and this occurs when corporations that don't really have an authentic company structure and activities in place meaning meeting minutes, board of directors, voting, etc.

Usually tactics like this are successful when there is poor management of company operations, meaning the co-mingling of personal funds and corporate funds, bad record keeping, mishandling allocations of money and really just using your company as a cash cow and scapegoat vehicle to escape taxes and potential penalties. If the plaintiff can prove to the judge that your company is nothing more than a front, than you could be in some serious trouble. But to avoid this you just need to keep everything above record and transparent and you shouldn't have anything to be fearful of.

Difference between S-Corp and C-Corp? You will have to discuss this in detail with you accountant, but I can give you a general overview. They are essentially the same, but they just differ in the way they are taxed and flexibility. S-corps are not taxed at the corporate level, but the shareholders of the company are taxed at the induvial level, and as for C-corps these business entities are taxed at the corporate level.

Real Estate & LLCs

If your getting into real estate I strongly suggest filling for a LLC (limited liability corporation) because of the immense tax advantages and protections that come with having a company as oppose to being an individual. My biggest piece of advise is when doing real estate have proper book keeping procedures in places because when dealing with the IRS they do not like when you co-mingle funds, especially if you open multiple LLCS and transfer money back and forth. Keep funds derived from your real estate portfolios separate, recorded, transparent and above board so they can't ding you with any penalizations.

Morals and Ethics For Long Term Success

Morals and ethics for long term success? What exactly do I mean by this? Well, believe it or not there are a lot of businesses out their that operate using shady tactics that really aggravate consumers and the tax man. Usually businesses like this don't last too long and are temporary, they generate some revenue, but after a short time cease to exist because they didn't follow fundamental moral and ethical business principles.

If you do not put your customers first and focus on enhancing customer's experiences how do you expect to thrive in the long run? For longevity you want repeat customers to consume your products or services, and if you give your customer base the shorter end of the stick you will lose out on the life time value of your customer.

You see a lot of businesses focus on acquiring more traffic by increasing the volume of their customer base as oppose to figuring out how they can add more value to current customers. How they can continue to serve current customers, enhance their experiences and be able to monetize them by providing more value. -This could be an upsell, cross-sell or whatever you want to call it.

For example, your in the weight loss niche, and your primary product is selling exercise equipment and workout routines, instead of trying to find more customers why don't you add recipe books, diet fads, custom meal creation, meal preps etc.? You see what I did here instead of looking for more customers to serve, I found another potential problem people could be struggling with and added value. Now You have customers buying not only exercise equipment and instructional workout videos, but you also have them buying your recipes and meal preps in tandem. You've easily doubled your monetization from one product or service to multiple.

Remember ensure you are truly serving your customer, and the old adage holds to be true "the customer is always right", and this couldn't be emphasized enough. When you start looking for your own selfish interest and not providing legendary service and high quality products focusing on enhancing customer experience you can expect your business to tapper off and become non-existent. Thus, the importance of morals and ethics, and also do not exaggerate the results of your product or services be honest and transparent. Give your customers realistic expectations and strive to overdeliver and not underdeliver.

Importance of Email Lists

I am sure you have heard of an email list? People say the "money is in the list", but what exactly is an email list? In this section of the book I will discuss the importance of building and maintaining your email list.

How do businesses sustain themselves over long periods of time and have the financial longevity that is so desired. Wealth that lasts and is almost timeless, and what does an email list have to do with any of this? Well, you see businesses don't just acquire customers they retain them, they become repeat buyers whom eventually become fans of your brand, product or services.

The email list is such an overlooked aspect to business and under utilized vehicle to monetize customers. I know some online marketers who have created robust and valuable lists that has made them a small fortune anytime they have launched a product or service, and I'm talking about tens of thousands of dollars just by sending out a single email that promote their products or services.

Hence, why I always tell people to create an email list and utilize it the right way! You don't want to come off spammy because one that will get your email blocked or end up in the spam folder, but you want to build rapport with your customer base and serve their needs. Give them freebies, everyone loves free stuff, promotional offers or discounts.

So don't only email them when you have something to sell. Have conversations with them ask them how they're doing, and the best thing you can do is actually ask them how they would like to be served? What kind of product or service would they like to see? – If you do this the right way I can tell you will be successful as long as you act accordingly. – Once you figure out what makes them tick and what they want, you can design the product/service accordingly and when your ready to launch there is an extremely high chance they will buy from you because your serving their needs.

The key here is you "know" your serving their needs vs you think you know what their needs are. Hence, the importance of communication with your email list. I seen so many times people trying to guess the needs of their customers only to have failed product/service launches.- Don't make that mistake.

I hope you see the potential power of email lists and how it can benefit your business regardless of what type of business you may have.

High Ticket

I don't know what stage your at in your business journey, perhaps your just starting out or maybe your trying to take things to the next level. Either way I wanted to discuss this important topic of "high ticket sales", and how this is a key component to financial freedom, stability and long lasting wealth.

You see whether you want to be a six figure earner, millionaire or even billionaire the concept of high ticket is very important to understand when your engaging in business. For instance, Michael Jordan and his top of the line premium shoes (that' how he markets them) retail on average for $250 dollars! – That's insane! $250 dollars for a pair of sneakers really? Now I am not here to debate whether that's something worth spending money on or not, but I wanted teach you something using this particular case study.

Michael Jordan realized that in order to maintain his wealth and stay rich he needs to acquire high ticket sales. How do you think he became a billionaire? I am sure it was more than just shoes, but his strategic and premium price point of his " Jordan" brand line had a big contribution to his success.

The fact is business boils down to a numbers game, and selling high ticket is essential to thrive and believe it or not it actually is less work! Think about it? Imagine selling a regular pair of sneakers that retails for $30 bucks and trying use marketing to promote them that runs you into $15 dollars per customer for marketing costs. Well guess what? There is already a problem - $15 dollars is already half of your selling price and is already eating into your profits!

What if you wanted to make $1000 dollars and lets say your cost per customer was $15 bucks meaning for every $30 you made per sale you spent $15 on marketing, thus your net profit is $15. ($30 sneaker price - $15 marketing = $15 dollars net profit)

How much would it take to get to $1000 dollars if your only making $15 bucks per sale? It would take you 67 pairs of sneakers to cross the $1000 dollars mark! Now let's look at the flipside of things, and if you were to sell Jordans using the average price point of $250. Let's say that marketing cost you more than double, let's say $50 dollars, so your cost per customer is $50 dollars for every pair of Jordans you sell, meaning that's a net profit of $200 dollars. ($250 Jordans price- $50 marketing cost = $200 net profit)

So how many pairs of Jordans would it take to hit the $1000 mark? **Only 5**! -That's right only 5 pairs of Jordans even if marketing costs were more than double! Now let's think about this logically and be pragmatic 5 pairs versus 67 pairs of shoes, which is easier to do? Obviously the 5 pairs of Jordans! You see this is the power of selling high ticket items and I just want to open your eye to help you see why high ticket is a tenet of the wealthy. In the previous section I discussed real estate, why do you think real estate is considered the game of the rich? I'll give you a hint its because real estate is essentially high ticket sales! Whether you're a real estate agent making high ticket commissions or an investor collecting rent, the name of the game is the same and it involves high ticket sales.

Of course Jordan has a lot of clout to back up his premium prices, undisputed one of the greatest to play the game of basketball, left a legacy and created his own brand based on himself. He was able to create a perceived value for the premium prices he charges and from a psychological stand point he did very well and succeeded. People are willing to spend over $200+ dollars on his shoes without question! Now that's what you called branding! Also, note the $250 dollar price range is his lower end sneakers.

Now its up to you to figure out how you can provide either a product or service that you are comfortable charging premium prices for.

Mindset

Before you even start getting into online businesses, stocks, real estate and pursuing the dream of passive income make sure you get your mindset right first! This section is going to be more of a self-development part of the book and is a crucial aspect to any and all businesses, which ever type you decide to go into.

You have to realize if your going to become wealthy you have to get your mindset right. You have to be willing to invest in yourself, education, equipment, incorporation fees, courses, etc. Remove any limiting belief systems that may be restraining you from moving forward. I use to struggle with a lot of limiting beliefs myself before I became a wealthy ***multi-millionaire***. – I came from a modest family and humble beginnings, I worked in the profession of security and wasn't being paid much, around $12 dollars an hour. Some months I worked 7 days a week! – I actually did this for half a year at one point in my life, but there came a point I realized that this was stupid!

I am spending 80% of my day working for somebody else making them richer, while I struggled to get by with a low paying job. I didn't want to spend my years grinding away to "work my way up the company" and work in some blue collar job eventually. I was just tired of working for someone else, being told what to do, when to leave and when I could go on vacations. I had an epiphany and that was if I was ever to become rich it wouldn't be working a typical 9-5 job. Although there are some extremely high paying sales jobs you can become relatively rich through, but flexibility to live life on your terms wouldn't be there.

So what did I do? I dared to dream and took that leap of faith invested in some online courses for online businesses (the ones I mentioned earlier) while working 7 days a week at security. My success wasn't overnight, but I grinded and in incremental steps I started to learn and advance and apply my knowledge and achieved success. Before you knew it I was making more money than I could ever make in security, and best of all it was mostly passive! So you probably guessed by now I gave in my 2 weeks for resignation to focus on these new online ventures and start building my wealth portfolio.

After I reached multiple six figures through various online business ventures (E-commerce, print on demand, publishing, video course creation, etc) I started to dive into the world of real estate, and started small with my first single family home. – I know I advised against this earlier, but I was starting out in real estate at the time. After accumulating 5 single family homes, cashflow positive, and combined with all my other online ventures, I was able to take a loan out and buy my first apartment complex that had 25 units. And from there the rest is history, I just rinsed and repeated the process and 10-31 exchanged my properties to keep building up my portfolio and defer taxes.

Before you knew it I was a multi-millionaire and to be honest it was surreal. It was just like yesterday I was working my security job watching the clock wind down awaiting my time to be relieved from my shift.

How did all this happen? It wasn't overnight, but took years of dedication and most of all the will to keep going and pursuing success until the bitter end. It wasn't all flowers and roses I faced a lot of obstacles, but was able to endure, recalibrate and overcome them. I don't credit my success to any accomplishments I've made alone, but with the community of like minded people I could sharpen myself with, my support systems. – My team.

Above all else I thank God for my success. I'm grateful for being able to do what I do, and taking my leap of faith. Success is a journey and will be filled with peaks and valleys, but as long as you can absorb failure and turn it into lessons learned you will be on your way to the mountain's peak. Its not an overnight thing, but takes incremental steps, sowing, grinding, tears, sweat and blood, patience, tenacity, and an analytical mind.

I can assure you good things do come for those that can find their way in the world of business. Following my advise in previous chapters and the following sub-chapters will definitely help in improving your current state of finances. These are the fundamentals to become wealthy, and to be quite honest there is no secrete formula apart from your own unique approach to creating a product or service for long term wealth creation.

Building Trust

What the art of selling really boils down to is the selling of "trust". But what do I mean by this? – You cannot sell an intangible attribute? Or can you? Well, to understand this we need to go beyond the surface level and take a deeper look at the mechanics of selling.

We know for the most part there are different types of buyers, we have impulse buyers, need buyers, seasonal buyers, bargain hunter buyers, and window shoppers.

Impulse Buyer – Buys things based on impulsive tendencies and doesn't really think things through, but tends to buy in bulk, especially online where one click check-outs are available. Or even at the mall when this buyer sees something appealing and buys at impulse without thinking it through.

Need Buyer- These are people who have problems and are looking for a solution. They know what they are looking for and have an idea of what they need to get, they have a motive before purchasing.

Seasonal Buyer – These are the kind of people you see at a specific time of year. Perhaps Summer, Autumn, Christmas, Halloween, Easter, etc. Any major seasonal shift attracts these types of buyers who buy within the transition of seasonal or social changes.

Barging Hunter – These are the toughest types of buyers to deal with they won't make a purchase without being able to acquire some sort of favorable deal, and tend to come out only when things are on sale. They want to get the best bang for their buck, and getting more for less is the type of mentality they operate under. These types of buyers get a sort of euphoric rush and feeling of validation when they purchase something of high perceived value for a lower cost.

Window Shopper Buyer – Arguably one of the hardest buyers to convert. These type of buyers are known to wander with no intentions and just observe. They may eventually purchase an item down the road, but usually takes a few weeks or even months after initial engagement.

So we know the difference types of buyers, but what does it mean to sell trust? It goes much deeper than the types of buyers and when you really break down the psychology behind this its not that complicated.

To sell trusts means you have built rapport and a sense of security, relationship is developed and authority or brand presence is front and center. Therefore, when your selling trust its based on a genuine relationship you developed.

For instance, when you buy from a specific sneaker brand or car brand such as Toyota or BMW although these are two different niche market brands they operate on the basis of selling trust.

Toyota – People buy Toyota because they know its reliable, fuel efficient and very low maintenance. I have a friend who still drives an old 2003 Toyota corolla that still functions in tip top condition with no problems at all since purchase. No extensive work needed to be done, only the typical oil change.

BMW- is more of a luxury brand, but the fact is they have built trust with their consumer base also. People flock to BMW knowing it's a trusted luxury brand that will deliver premium quality without fail.

So how is trust built? I have outlined the following general steps that are used to build trust

7 Steps to Building Trust:

1. Creating awareness.
2. Serving your defined customer avatar's needs.
3. Deliver high perceived value to the marketplace.
4. Transparency.
5. Building rapport & customer engagement.
6. Establishing Authority & Presence in your niche.
7. Trust is built.

If you follow my 7 trust building steps I am sure you will find success. It takes time to build trust, but when you invest in this endeavor you won't be disappointed. -This is how Kylie Jenner sold $900 million from her product line launch! How? She built trust! Without trust no business can be sustained in the long term nor produce real wealth. Hence, I emphasize the importance of building trust because trust precedes the money. If you focus on building trust with a high quality product or service, serve your audience and create a tribe the money will follow.

Remember money or wealth is a by product of your success. When you solely focus on money and selfish motives you won't be able to have true wealth and longevity.

I have a Jewish friend who's a very successful business man, and he also believes in the tenet of selling "trust", rather than just selling products or services. He tells me people always want to do business with him because he has built trust and when he makes a lot of money they also make a lot of money too. Hence, wealth is shared and distributed.

I hope you gained some in depth insights on this section. Trust is an extremely important aspect to any business deal because you wouldn't do business with someone you didn't trust!

I have a friend who created an online course, and of course he had a track record that gave him clout. But watch this, he spent the first 6 months building "trust" on YouTube creating his following. He basically used the 7 steps to building success, and guess what?

On launch day he cashed in over **30k+ USD!** How did he achieve such an incredible feat in one day? Let's take a closer look and analyze my 7 steps to building trust.

1. He created awareness. He let his audience know that there were other ways to create passive income online to help you become finically independent.
2. He defined who his customers were right out of the gate. In a way he screened/prequalified them by staying laser focus in his specific niche.
3. He over delivered in value and just outworked everyone in his space.
4. He was 100% transparent. No sneaky upsells or cross sells just pure honesty.
5. He took time to build rapport and actually answered his audience's questions and built genuine relationships. Engagement was there.
6. Built authority showing that he was an expert and had a large presence in the space.
7. Trust was built and thus he pulled the trigger by launching his course monetizing his fan base.

Do you see how beautifully that worked? This guy's YouTube channel wasn't even that big it was under 5k subscribers, but he built trust the right way. As a result he was rewarded for his hard work and cashed in over 30k in one day! I should also note he used all the business principles I discussed, such as selling his product for high ticket value, ethics, trust, email lists, etc .

Volume Vs Margins

There are two types of businesses. Businesses that take the route of volume and businesses that uphold margins. But what exactly does this mean? Well, here's the thing some businesses operate under the principles of pushing large volume of transactions to become wealthy.

While other businesses follow another model which is selling high ticket and keeping costs down and sales high. These are almost polar opposite styles of businesses, but each one has its merits. It does come down to preference to be honest, but I personally prefer margins over volume. Why you may ask? Its just more efficient and less work!

Do you remember earlier the example I provided about selling a regular pair of sneakers vs Jordans? Do you remember the amount of shoes I would need to sell to get to $1000 for each pair of sneakers? The results were astronomically different and that example displayed volume vs margins. The regular pair of sneakers used volume to reach $1000, but Jordans required much less transactional volume and leveraged margins.

These two types of business models engage in two totally different type of customers. One customer is more low ticket, while the other one is more niche and willing to divvy out more money for a pair of shoes. Understanding your customers is also essential for long term success. You wouldn't want to sell Jordans to a customer who's willing to only pay $30 for a pair of shoes, and a customer willing to spend over $200+ is not interested in a normal pair of shoes.

There is nothing inherently wrong with either business models or customers. But just understand each paradigm serves a different type of customer one is low ticket (normal) and the other is high ticket (niche). Understanding your customer's desires will help you develop a more comprehensive monetization business strategy that you can use to maximize your profits.

Secrete To Creating Success & Misconceptions

What is the secrete sauce or magic formula to success? What if I told you there is none, and what a lot of financial experts and gurus tell you are complete lies. Its all smoke and mirrors. We must understand a few things in order to achieve success, we must grasp what precedes success and debunk myths and misconceptions.

Bring value to the marketplace! The marketplace will determine your value, focus on solving problems, bringing forth solutions to people's everyday problems. The market wants what the market wants and doesn't care if your passionate about anything. – I want to reiterate this last point and that is the market doesn't CARE what your passionate about.

People want their needs met that's why they shop in the first place its either for a solution to a problem or to be entertained. You wouldn't believe how many times I see naive entrepreneurs on YouTube trying to start their own channel only to fall face first and fail. They didn't do their due diligence or research, creating travel vlogs that plain suck or having no value to give is why they fail.

If you cannot entertain your audience, than I suggest doing something that solves their problems. I know I'm being blunt, but this needs to be established because there are so many misconceptions people believe.

This is business 101 supply and demand, find a need in a niche and do your best to serve that market segment and the money will follow. Nobody cares how passionate you are, your personal agenda, etc. People want to be served, remember 95% of the world are consumers while 5% are content creators. You need to step into the perspective of the 5% and figure out ways to add value and serve your customer avatar. It's as simple as that there is no black hat tricks, hacks, or any wizardry at work, but good old fashion hard work.

Niche Down & Laser Focus

Why do some businesses fail while other seem to thrive? The importance of niching down and staying laser focused is a subject not often talked about in the realm of business. So what exactly does this mean? You see to many people try to do everything and try to be the next "Wal-Mart", although that is an extremely profitable business model the fact is not everybody can do this as it requires immense man power, serious logistic management, resources and a lot of capital.

To often I see businesses fall into a generalization where they don't really have a specific market to serve or let alone identify who their customer avatar is. The danger of this is when your business is to general and has no specific purpose to serve your audience you will not acquire customers because you haven't identified their specific needs.

I am not talking about surface level business delivery of products/services, but you must go deep under layers of layers and really hone in on what your business specializes in.

So for example you want to get into health/fitness a very saturated niche and also extremely competitive. I see business owners taking the broad stroke of the brush and decide they will get into teaching yoga classes. There's problems with this decision already, one yoga is not niched down enough, two customer base has not been defined, three there are no other monetization strategies in places to maximize revenue.

Now I'll show you the right approach to creating a successful yoga business.

1. Niched down to teach "hot yoga"
2. Yoga For women only between ages 18-50
3. Sell Yoga mats, tights, attire, etc

Do you see the difference? I narrowed down to a more less competitive market, hot yoga, which I also specified the target audience whom are women between ages 18-50 years of age. On top of that I created additional monetization strategies by including the selling of desired yoga products along side with the monthly yoga fees.

That's how you niche down and stay laser focused on what your doing. When I say laser focus I mean your specifically serving that niche and you are not dabbling in any other businesses. In business you have to remain focused, sound minded and have the ability to make critical decisions. You kind of have to be like our ancestors who had to hunt for food for survival, and what are the traits of hunters? They remained laser focused, stalked their prey, and executed a ferocious attack until their goal was achieved.

This is what it means to niche down and stay laser focused. I hope you've learned something valuable from this section that you can apply to your business or even personal life.

Why Online Businesses Are The Best Way To Start Out?

Why do I recommend starting out with the online business model? I truly believe were living in one of the greatest times in regards to the abundance of opportunity for starting your own online venture. We live on a planet of over 7 billion people, and only a small percentage of people have access to the internet here in the industrialized world. But soon that will change within 10 years time , at least 1 billion more people will flood the net, and that means you potentially have more customers to serve.

Most the hard work is already done for you. If you join as an affiliate or partner with any major companies such as Shopify, T-spring, Etsy, etc you can just easily leverage off the warm traffic that is there. When you partner with other corporation's platforms you get easy traffic, customers with the intent to buy your product or services are already present.

It doesn't get any better or any easier than that. All the heavy lifting is done for you, and all you have to do is come up with a product that serves the audience.

With Online business models you have the potential to make leveraged or "passive income" which you couldn't do with conventional businesses. If you started a conventional business you would have to do all the hard work yourself, market and somehow drive traffic to your product, manage employees, logistics, etc.

But because your utilizing the online web you don't have to worry about any of that stuff! Work is still required, but not at the level of a traditional business. An additional perk to having your business online is you get what is called location mobility, and as long as you have a secure internet connection anywhere around the world you can work! – Yes, that means you can work with nothing but your underwear on at home with a laptop. When you go on vacation you can simply manage your business from the resort's WIFI connection.

Last but not least is when you operate an online business you get to connect to a global economy! The scalability is endless you get to access new potential customers all across the globe and transcend time zones because your business technically runs 24/7, meaning you can even make money while you sleep!

Imagine waking up to new sales or perhaps you have an errand to run and you get a notification of more orders being filled for a certain product. This is the power of having an online business and if used correctly can definitely enhance the quality of your life.

I like to compare online businesses and passive income to valleys and peaks on a continuum of hills. Imagine you have to push a car or cart up a hill, at first its very hard trying to set the ground work trying to establish the foundational framework. But once you get it to the peak of the hill what happens? It starts going down hill by itself automatically and when it reaches the bottom of the valley it starts to climb itself back up with the previous momentum, and than you come in and have to push the car or cart up again, and than rinse and repeat the process.

If you haven't grasped the picture I am trying to paint I will elaborate. So the initial effort of pushing the car or cart up-hill is when you get started out learning the ropes and just trying to figure things out. But once you get the hang of it you start to create what is called "passive income", but after a few months of passive income you start to notice your income is declining due to you not continuing to put work in.

So after you realize this you start to get back to work and continue with the momentum you left off with. – The good news is you don't start from rock bottom as you established the foundation.

Hence, a few months of hard work are followed by a few months of passive income if done correctly. You just continue to rinse and repeat the process.

My message is essentially now is the best time to get started with any online venture as the opportunities are endless.

The Importance Of Surveying Your Audience

What is the relevance of surveying your audience? Why do your research and due diligence before investing into launching a product or services? This is arguably one of the most important tenets to business if not the most important. All to often I see young entrepreneurs diving into things blindly failing to research there target demographic and not defining who exactly they are serving.

I see this happening all the time and hence why a lot of entrepreneurs don't make it past the first year and go back to their 9-5s. They fail a crucial component of business, which is researching before even getting started. Why on earth would someone invest time, energy, and money on something you have not researched and have no proof of concept?

Its beyond me why someone would take such a bold risk without doing their due diligence. Business is not guess work or a matter of "hoping". Business at the end of the day is a numbers game and is based on facts. You base things and move accordingly to the information you gathered through reconnaissance. With business there will always be a certain degree of uncertainty and risk, but you want to take measured risks.

There's a big difference between a measured risks and a blatant blind risk with oversight. Hence, the importance of sharpening your mind and self-education through proper financial education. You want to see things on a deeper level and not just scratch the surface. In the end experience will be your teacher, and learning from the mistakes of others who've come before you can save you a lot of time.

Bottom line before starting a new venture please do your due diligence and take all the necessary precautions needed to proceed, mitigate risk, and become successful.

Figuring out your Why?

So you probably decided to read this book to learn about different ways to make passive income and educate yourself with solid business foundational principles. But have you figured out your why?

Have you figured out the reason why you truly want to get into making a passive income and start your own online enterprise? Perhaps, you want another side hustle, spend more time with the family, live life on your terms or travel the world and experience life more in abundance?

Maybe its to create a legacy, impact the lives of people worldwide, innovating or inventing new methods? Whatever your why is make sure its strong enough to stand the test of times because any investment comes with its own obstacles.

This is just my opinion, but I believe the strongest "why" you can have is more altruistic in nature and is something that benefits others more than it benefits your own interests. What do I mean by that?

When people who live for a greater purpose it usually means your serving the world and have other's best interests in mind. Remember how I said money or wealth is by-product of the trust you create and the value you bring to the marketplace? In that same way your personal interests such as traveling, material things, etc are all by-products of the value you bring to the world. – Think of it as a reward.

You are free to adopt any perspective you want that will help you survive long term in business, but I personally believe an altruistic, devoted and humble purpose is the best driving force to have. I am speaking from experience as there was a point in my life where I was driven by material things, fast women, status, prestige, expensive dinners, popularity, etc. But all these things fade and brought no true happiness in my life, but it wasn't until I shifted my mentality to a more altruistic purpose in life I started to truly cherish and embellish meaning to my life.

I don't want you to make the same mistakes I did, so I admonish you to figure out your why before getting started with anything.

Knowing The Different Between Liabilities And Assets

Believe it or not most the general public are illiterate when it comes to understanding the difference between liabilities and assets. There is a reason why the rich are getting richer and the poor is growing poorer, and the gap is continuing to grow bigger and bigger.

Poor people tend to buy liabilities while rich people buy assets that generate positive cashflow. For instance, if I was to give $1000 to someone with a poor mindset and $1000 to a person with a rich mindset what do you think would happen? Let's say in this scenario both individuals start off on the same socioeconomic bracket in life.

I can assure you that person #1 with the poor mindset will accumulate liabilities that depreciate in value. Perhaps he buys the best designer clothes, new sneakers, jewelry, etc. On the other hand person #2 with the rich mindset uses his money more prudently and starts his own LLC business and than uses the rest of the money as capital to fund his business endeavors.

As you can see in the example I've drawn out for you how different poor people think versus how rich people think. Poor people tend to think and live in the moment, while the rich have more of a long term vision and focus on wealth creation and longevity. Money tends to gravitate towards those who can keep it, attract it and multiply it.

There's an old African proverb that says give a man a fish and he eats for a day, but teach a man to fish and he eats for a life time. The poor tend to have this acquired helplessness mindset and attitude towards life, and have a strong sense of entitlement. But the rich want to educate themselves and learn how to leverage systems and make money work for them.

The poor work for money while the rich make money work for them. Poor people considered cars, houses, and designer clothing assets, while the rich consider them liabilities. Although an argument can be made that cars used for uber or rental houses are assets, but in this scenario I'm referring to houses that people live in that cost you monthly expenses and don't generate you cashflow, and a luxury car that is just sitting in the garage and is only used for social status.

So I want you to practice in your mind whenever you have leisure time to become more self-aware and identify assets and liabilities within your life. The simple rule of thumb to identify assets and liabilities is if its either costing you money (liability) or making you money(asset). Perhaps this will help give you a better financial assessment of your current state of affairs. Simple right?

Abundance Vs Scarcity Mindset

Mindset is another crucial component in business that isn't talked about nearly enough. The fact is if you want to become wealthy you need to change certain mannerisms, ideologies or concepts of money you have been mislead to believe through your upbringing.

You need to start thinking like a business man or women, and not an employee. Here's the thing the world is filled with opportunity, and despite what the news tells you that there's not enough, limited resources, limited opportunities, etc.- That is simply not the truth. This all comes from people plagued with scarcity mentalities.

You have to be cognizant that the world is a big place and the opportunities are almost infinite you just need to find them. Leave behind your thinking of negativity, fears and insecurities. You can have your piece of the pie in this global market and become wealthy you just have to work for it. Especially with the advent of the internet this has brought an explosion of growth and opportunities for you to take advantage of.

Never before have we in the history of mankind become so interconnected and intergraded on a global scale that we can communicate to one another at the push of a button. Its just an incredible time to be alive in and its really up to you to cease the opportunity.

Imagine having a glass of water filled half way and now its up to you to decide if that glass is half empty or half full? Those stuck in the scarcity mindset view the glass as half-full because opportunities are always running out for them. But those who think in abundance realize that there is always room for more growth, thus the glass is half empty. – The question is which perspective do you think from and why?

Ultimately its your choice to choose which mindset you will operate under. I can only point you in the right direction. This doesn't only apply to business it could be applied to relationships, politics, and other global affairs as well.

The Truth About Debt & Credit

What is the truth about Debt? This is a real controversial topic and depending what end of the spectrum you've had exposure to will determine the perspective you hold. I'll be the first to say that this is a very "grey" area topic and its not black and white as most people make out to be.

Pioneers of the varying philosophies behind abstaining from getting into debt or using credit as a means of wealth creation are polar opposite. These different guiding principles to wealth stem from **Dave Ramsey** & **Robert Kiyosaki** whom both have been scrutinized by many financial gurus, analysts and have captured international attention.

Dame Ramsey's Philosophy - Is very practical and conservative. Admonishing people NOT to use credit cards, stay out of debt, and save, save, save! Make conservative investments into dividends, bonds, and even real estate. But his approach is not necessarily for those who aim for true wealth creation, but are more so for the middle class and blue collar worker. Playing with debt is like playing with fire.

***Robert Kiyosaki's 's Philosophy*-**   This unique and very controversial approach has caught a lot of criticism going against conventional wisdom like Dave Ramsey's teachings, and actually advises people to get into debt to get rich. Also, advises instead of saving money for small long term profits, instead you should find ways to borrow other people's money, using credit from banks and use the funds to purchase assets that create positive cashflow on a monthly recurring basis, ideally real estate investments.

This type of philosophy is based on the assumption you have a good financial education and can discern the difference between an asset and liability, basically being able to identify what puts money into your pocket and what takes money out of your pocket. More of an advanced thinking and is for those who looking to establish big wealth creation portfolios. This type of thinking has been adopted widely and is popular among entrepreneurs, investors, and other business tycoons.

More specifically where Kiyosaki's philosophy shines is in regards to identifying if your house is an asset or liability, and he points out if your living in your house despite how much equity may be built into it if its causing you to lose cash meaning mortgage payments, property taxes, utilities, repairs and fixes, etc. Than your house is NOT a asset, but is actually a liability. He points out that this is determined by where the "cash flows", and thus since the cashflow's outside of your pockets it should be considered a liability. On the other hand if your using a rental property and the cash is flowing into your pockets, than it's a asset.

Now your probably wondering ok well both these business philosophies are quite convincing, but which one do I choose to live by? Both Ramsey and Kiyosaki have made good arguments and have track records to back their statements up.

Well, the answer isn't clear cut or simple because in actual fact I would advise to live by both! You see both these business principles are effective and do hold to be true for the most part, but the question is what do you want from life? If you desire to just get by in life and have no dreams of bigger things, than I recommend you listen to Dave Ramsey. However, if you feel like there is more for you out there in what life has to offer and your looking for long lasting wealth I suggest you take the latter approach (Kiyosaki's philosophy).

I am personally a big proponent of Robert Kiyosaki's teaching as mainstream conventional wisdom is absolutely wrong and quite frankly don't know what their talking about when it comes to money. My personal financial philosophy is more synergistic and utilizes both ideologies.

You see what Dave Ramsey got right was that you shouldn't take debt or use credit to buy things you don't have money for in the first place. This is absolutely undisputable fact, and there's an ancient proverbial saying to go along with that which is "the borrower is servant to the lender", however what Ramsey missed and failed to see was that you can leverage debt to get rich, especially in the world of real estate. People find ways to get approved for big loans from the bank and purchase rental properties that provide recurring cashflow on a monthly basis and thus the investment pays off the debt you have by itself. – There are real estate tycoons who use this strategy and are in debt of upwards to millions upon millions of dollars and of course have used this large sum of money to fund their real estate investments.

The take away that I want to bring to you is quite simple and that's do not use debt or credit to buy your luxuries and unessential needs, but instead leverage debt to buy asset generating investments such as real estate or any other positive cashflow producing wealth vehicle. The poor get into debt to buy their luxuries, while the rich rent them or have created enough wealth to own them.

– This is an observation I have made and it holds to be true even today.

How To Use Debt To Create Wealth

You are probably wondering ok I know that debt can be used to create wealth, but how exactly do I do this? I will touch on this and elaborate on how you too can use debt to create wealth. First off, if your looking to get approved from any lender whether banks, private investors, etc. There are few key considerations that come into play when you submit your application for a big loan.

Key Points of Consideration

1. Do you have the capacity to pay them back? Lenders will look at your income, assets, and other liabilities such as money you may owe other creditors. These factors will determine the amount of money they can service you.

2. How much capital do you have? Lenders will look at how much capital you can put forth whether it's a purchase for a house, business etc. This could also mean your savings, and equity, they want to see what you can potentially liquidate for cash.

3. Contingency plan. They want to know if your plans fail to pan out whether that be a house investment, start-up tech company or any other business venture that they have security and will have the means to be paid back. This is also known as collateral.

4. Conditional points. When accepting a loan or mortgage there will be special conditions put in place, and this means the type of interest you are going to be paying, line of credit, fixed loans, and lending value ratios which is the amount of the loan you will be utilizing, and also what your exit strategy will be. Each loan has different variables and is looked at by a case by case situation.

5. Track record. Lenders look at your track record when determining your eligibility to be approved for any loan, meaning how is your job retention? Do you frequently change job occupations? How is your credit score? Do you pay your bills on time? Do you owe any other creditors money? Also, most importantly how much applications have you submitted within a six month period. – If you have applied for a lot of loans and got rejected it won't look good on you as it shows the lender you are desperate for money and don't have the means to pay it back, not only

that but applying for credit too often can hurt your credit score!

Now you know the 5 key considerations I want to give you a case study to show you how using debt to create wealth looks like when implemented. -Assuming you are approved the loan and you decide to invest into a rental property. A property is purchased for 200k and after all your expenses including property, tax, insurance, closing costs, you profit 30k. So every passing year your tenants are paying down your mortgage month after month, thus you build what is called equity. After you build your equity to about 20 or 30 thousand dollars you go back to the bank and ask for another loan for another property valued at 450k.

Again, the bank will look at the 5 key considerations I mentioned, and assuming you were a good steward with managing the money you were initially given for the first loan, than they will approve you for this 450k loan. Assuming you replicate the same results as your initial investment property you just rinse and repeat the process again and again. This is the wealth formula that the rich use to become wealthy and maintain their status.

Bad Credit- What Should I Do?

There could be various reasons why you have bad credit perhaps you have been a victim of fraud or your just simply bad at managing your personal finances. Usually it's the latter because generally speaking the average persons is not very good at being a good steward of his/her finances. This is actually quite common as the everyday person isn't taught a proper financial education when they're in school. Financial literacy is at an all time low for the "average joe", and the school system isn't doing anything about it! – Upgrading your financial intuition is probably why you purchased this book in the first place, right?

Its actually quite shocking students graduating from institutions designed for higher education no nothing about taxes, finances and investing. The sad thing is we live in a monetary world where money governs almost everything we do, hence it would be prudent to have a solid financial IQ. From being employed by a company, buying groceries, booking flights for travel, and acquiring your first house all encompass the common denominator "money". Yet, our school system has failed us in properly educating the masses about financial literacy, but encourage students to take arbitrary programs to major in with no guarantee of a job or financial stability. On the contrary students amass huge loans only to regret their decision of pursuing higher education.

Of course there are majors that can make you a good living in life and those professions encompass law, science, accounting, engineering, and even going into trade school.

So you have bad credit, but what is the remedy? The first thing is the most obvious you need to look at your spending habits. If your spending money on liabilities or perhaps living above your means than you have some serious problems. How much money do you put aside to re-invest in your financial education? – I am not talking about conventional education like going to university, however I'm referring to books like mine that cost less than a fraction of university. How much books have you read in the past six months on financial literacy? Do you put money aside for "rainy days" or just blow it all in one go? – At the least you should have at the minimum of six months of living expense in your savings account, which should only be touched in case of emergencies. The majority of people live pay cheque to pay cheque and the scary thing is if they were to lose their job the next day they would probably be living on the streets! Hence, the importance of having contingency funds in place in case of emergencies.

Do you have money tied up in stocks, bonds, or mutual funds? What action have you taken to better yourself financially? Did you know the number 1 reason marriages fall apart in America is due to financial instability! – That's right not adultery, but simply because couples cannot get their finances right and get into a lot trouble. Let's face the fact that getting your money right is an important tenet in life and a lot of people just don't take this seriously enough. That's why its your responsibility to educate yourself and enhance your financial intelligence. Its so sad to see marriages fall apart because people think that good feelings, attraction, and being nice to each other is enough to get you through life! – But they are sadly mistaken!

Now your probably thinking ok I am aware of my bad spending habits, living above my means, not saving, and not investing in my financial education has lead me to this rut, but what can I do to start fixing my bad credit? You hear a lot of supposed "experts" giving out advise like keep your credit utilization down, use your credit card to build good credit history, use secure or pre-paid credit cards. – But we know these basic remedies won't work, you probably don't have the cash on hand to get a secured credit card, and you can't get either good credit history or credit utilization low because you don't have access to a credit card. This is sort of a catch 22, but what can you actually do to fix your bad credit dilemma?

Well, the only way your going to get this fixed if your at rock bottom is you will have to ***dispute*** all the negative things and these adverse accounts entail off your credit report. How do you do this? – Write a credit dispute letter! "Section 609" of the fair credit report act states that the letter you send is not contingent on if the adverse account is valid or not, however, this letter is your right to dispute the adverse accounts on your credit report which credit agencies have recorded.

So what this means is in your letter you are questioning if the credit reporting agency has the right to report adverse accounts on your credit history. – The thing is these credit reporting agencies need to maintain a signed document from you in order to have these adverse accounts present on your credit report. Thus, they need to prove without a shadow of a doubt if these adverse accounts truly belong to you. If they do not have this signed document from you, than they must delete all your adverse accounts! Ergo, if they don't have this signed document from you they have to remove it. This strategy I advise is directed towards those of you living in America, and not abroad as I don't know how the credit system works in other countries.

Your probably wondering what do the content of these credit dispute letters entail? I am going to provide you a template for you to use, now I can't guarantee you this will work 100% of the time, but I can tell you it has worked for many people I know.

Dispute Letter Template:

Your Full Name:

Address: (current)

SSN

DOB (Date of birth)

Date

Dear _____ (creditor name)

I would like to request for an investigation for the account listed below as it has not reflected accurately on my credit report.

Creditor Account(s):

I dispute this account with all 3 credit bureaus, and have stated the account has been verified by your company. This is incorrect, thus I am requesting your company to investigate the matter further and correct the inaccurate account information. The law from section 623 (a)(8) states the right for a consumer which enables me to request for an investigation. Please advise.

Kind Regards,

Signature:

The key take away to the dispute letter is your contacting the creditor or creditors and are requesting for an investigation to take place on the account in question. Than you quote the fair credit reporting act law 623 (a)(8) and advise them it is your right as a consumer request an investigation to rectify any inaccurate inconsistencies on the account.

Again, I can't guarantee you that all your adverse accounts will be reversed as there is a bunch of factors in play such as your credit history, type of creditor, and what stage your at with your creditors. But, this can be worth a try as I have mentioned I know a lot of people this has worked for.

Conclusion

You've reached the end of this book and I hope you learned something new whether it was about day trading options, dividends, real estate, passive income and foundational business principles. You'll notice all these vehicles to wealth encompass similar themes, but at the same time can be very different in there approach.

If there was one message I wanted to drive home to you after completing this book that's there are no short cuts to long lasting wealth. Short cuts, loop holes, black-hat tricks or whatever you want to call them, these don't last and if your trying to create a sustainable business model and long term wealth creation, than you need to have the proper mindset and work ethic in place.

Focus on premium quality products or services and deliver outstanding customer engagement, build trust because remember at the end of the day your actually selling trust. Meaning people are trusting your brand and the products or services it entails.

Whatever business model you decide to choose just remember "Rome wasn't built in a day", anything worthwhile will require you to invest a lot of your time and energy. You must have the mindset that your building an empire and empires are not built overnight, but take time and dedication to be completed.

Beware scams and gurus that smile claiming you can create permanent passive income and retire on the beach of Bali sipping martinis for the rest of your life. The reality is that this is nothing but a myth. What you don't focus on will eventually decline, and thus turn your passive income to no income at all. Hence, a better way of looking at it is you have leveraged income that must be maintained accordingly.

Don't forget there is no "I" in business. You can only keep it solo for so long, but when you get to the point of expansion you must start either to team up with partners, outsource or hire employees to work under you. The greatest companies in existence are not "one man operations" or "lone-wolves", but have a team of people working together in unison. Humility is key because understanding that you can't become successful alone is when you start to grasp the fact that no man or women is an island, and we are all dependent on each other to survive. For instance, even when I started out although I managed much of my day to day operations by myself, I still had a team that consisted of lawyers, accountants, graphic designers, freelancers, virtual assistants, etc.

I wish you the best in your future endeavours and hope you apply what you've learned. Remember Success is like a muscle you got to keep working it out! -Even on the days you don't feel like your going anywhere, you just keep pushing!

Best Wishes,

Jason Morgan

Jason Morgan